Lost Angel Unleashed

Stories from the Heart
By, Linda Ballou

WIND DANCER PRESS

Wind Dancer Press

Editor: Barbara Milbourn
Layout by www.formatting4U.com

Digital ISBN: 978-1-7379253-5-4
Print ISBN: 978-1-7379253-4-7
Published in 2023 in the United States
Wind Dancer Press

Love recognizes no barriers.

~ Maya Angelou

What Readers are saying about Lost Angel Unleashed!

"You know you're in for a wild ride from the opening passages of Linda Ballou's new collection of travel stories titled *Lost Angel Unleashed*. The book is filled with as riotous tales as the scary plane ride she endures in the first story. Each story here has its own charm. Each is a little nugget of literary deliciousness."

- AJ Llewellyn, Mystery Author

"Lost Angel Unleashed is a scrumptious read. You may find that it is tempting to rush through it, just for the pleasure of letting your eyes "gulp down" Linda's beautifully descriptive prose. Read it at a more sedate pace, so that you can really take in all the delightful details she masterfully crafts into each story."

- Anne Holmes, CEO-National Association of Baby Boomer Woman

"The author has been very personal and shared who she is and how she became the brave woman she is today."

- Terry Lister, author of West Africa Travel narratives

"Written to inspire you to get off the couch throw the clicker out the window, and find you own adventures. Ballou's attention to detail enables the reader to visualize the places described vividly, evoking a sense of wanderlust and a desire to embark on a new adventure."

- DJ Adamson, author of
Lillian Dove Mystery series

"I was intrigued by her earlier books, and now I think this one, a brave, tell-all collection of events and places that most influenced her life surpasses her earlier books. She embraces the remote places and unusual people she encountered along the way."

- Bonnie Neely, Founding Editor of
Real Travel Adventure e-zine and author of
Real Ventures: Did We Really Do That?

"Linda Ballou faces her fears directly scrambling through unchartered landscapes. If you want to learn about this brave wild seeking adventurer, Linda shares her remarkable stories from the heart in *Lost Angel Unleashed*."

- Shannon D. Fit Life Travel

Contents

Introduction

I am a lost angel living among 17 million others in Los Angeles. Southern California has served me well as a springboard to great adventures for over 30 years. I love the California Coast and have taken great pleasure in exploring the grandeur of sometimes rugged, but always beautiful interface with the grand and vibrant sea. In *Lost Angel in Paradise,* I shared 32 of my favorite day trips from Malibu to Mendocino. In my first travel collection, *Lost Angel Walkabout*, I gathered my most meaningful and transformative travel experiences from the beginning of my travel writing career to 2010. *Lost Angel Unleashed* reveals some of the more personal stories that I did not feel comfortable sharing until now. In *Bear Heart*, I explain how the trajectory for me to become a travel writer was in place long before I had any notion of becoming one. Over the years I have returned to my hometown of Haines, Alaska many times. Like a spawning salmon, I search for peace in the headwaters of my youth.

This book includes travel memoirs from the way-back machine, as well as recent adventures. I wrote **Trains on Fire** when I was 25 on my way to a summer session in England. There are essays on how a travel experience affected me. **Too Many Elephants in the Room** may offend some sensibilities as Western travelers' sympathies lie with the elephants ravaged by poachers rather than with the people who must live with them. Just before the Covid shutdown I was in Australia. Serendipity took me to the **Que Station** where I learned about the severe measures taken to quell the spread of the Spanish flu that struck in 1912.

Part Two of this book details destinations that were so wonderful that I wanted to share them with readers. I hope to inspire you to get off the couch, throw the clicker out the window, and find your own adventures. My parting thought to you is that we can find salvation in nature.

I hope this offering is worthy of your precious time on our ever-evolving planet.

Part One

Thanks for the Memories

Bear Heart

I leaned into a cold wind whipping up off the tiny boat harbor of Haines, Alaska on my way home from school. I arrived to find my father strapping the last bit of mailing tape around two boxes containing my belongings. I was to go on a trip that would change my life for better, or for worse, forever. I was fourteen and had never gone anywhere on my own.

"Get your jacket. The plane is waiting for you," he growled.

"What plane?" I asked, horrified.

"The mail plane. I already talked to the pilot. You are leaving here today."

"Where am I going?" I looked over to my mother who stared at me with a helpless look in her eyes.

"You are going to stay with Grandma Fry," she said in a voice that was barely audible.

Grandma Fry was not my grandmother. She was a kindly old woman who lived in a creaking shack surrounded by a jungle of plants. My mother used to go to her house to get clippings when we lived in California.

3

But I don't even know Grandma Fry," I whimpered in protest.

"It doesn't matter. You are out of here today," my father replied.

He scooped up my bundled belongings and put them in the cab of our truck and told me to get in. The instant my door shut, he gunned the engine, and we were off. As he sped past the Pioneer Bar, I could make out a few regulars sipping their whiskeys on the rocks. I wondered which one of them told my father they saw me with Bobby after I'd been warned never to see him again.

As my father drove towards the airport beneath a lowered Alaskan sky, we passed by the Moose Horn Café where the other kids were huddled over hot chocolates. Rain splattered the windshield as we continued past the high school. The wipers worked overtime as the truck bounced through mud puddles in the road pocked with frost boils. By the time we arrived at the airstrip, the drizzle had turned to downpour. The pilot was waiting with the engine warmed up but expressed reservations about flying that day. Mail for Haines was (and still is) often held in Juneau, ninety miles to the south, for days because the planes are socked in due to soggy weather.

"Why do I have to go today?" I mustered the courage to ask.

"You've been with that black bastard again," my father hissed into the wolf ruff of his parka. Anyone who did not share his pasty pallor was considered inferior.

Bobby wasn't black. He was a half-Tlingit Indian, of Mongolian descent, with a broad forehead, dark almond-shaped eyes, prominent cheekbones, and mocha-colored skin. He wasn't a bastard either. His mother was an Indian from the native village of Klukwan resting on the Chilkat River. It has been there for two hundred years, long before my father's arrival. Bobby's father was a fisherman who happened to be white. Mark Twain said, "Travel is fatal to prejudice, bigotry, and narrow-mindedness." Too bad my dad didn't get around a bit more. His attitude might have changed.

"It doesn't look good, Mat," the pilot said, leaning out of the plane and holding up the plastic window flapping in the wind.

"I really want her out of here today," my father said. In his mind, he felt he was doing the right thing because he was saving my life. If I didn't get out of his sight today, there was a strong chance he might do something he would regret—something like strangling his darlin' daughter with his bare hands.

The pilot taxied down the airfield dotted with patches of glare ice. The visibility was nil. He taxied back to where my father and I were waiting for his verdict.

"I really don't think it's a good idea, Mat," he yelled out his window over the wind.

I knew my life was in serious jeopardy when my father replied, "Give it a go."

He tossed my bags in the plane and helped lift me into the back seat. My trembling sobs held no sway.

"Buckle up," came from the pilot. "Don't worry little lady. I've made this flight a million times. It's just going to be a little bumpy today," he added with skeptical bravado as he revved the engine. We taxied down the runway smothered beneath an iron curtain of clouds. In moments we lifted off and were plying our way to Juneau over the Lynn Canal. Rain splattered on the windows as the plane tossed from side to side in the stiff winds. I was weeping silently into the fur of my parka, trying to get a grip when the plane dropped what seemed like ten stories in two seconds. I bounced so high I hit my head on the ceiling of the plane. Shaken to the core, I was scared speechless. But it didn't matter. My screams could not be heard over the din of the engine anyway.

The pilot craned his head around the seat to see if I was okay. "Why don't you come up here?" he asked. "You can help me fly this buggy."

I welcomed anything to get my mind off impending doom. I wiggled between the seats and joined him in the tiny cockpit. He took my hand into his calloused paw and squeezed hard. "This here is a float plane. If I had to, I could put us down right here on the canal. It's going to be okay. Don't you worry none."

He told me to take hold of the half-wheel moving about in front of my seat.

"Now, if you want to learn how to fly you couldn't have a better lesson than today," he laughed.

My stomach calmed and tears subsided as I grabbed hold of the wheel and concentrated on becoming an ace pilot. We chugged through a solid gray mass of clouds with blinding rain pelting the window for what seemed an eternity. Occasionally the wind would lift a wing and tip us like a kite off balance. The pilot would bring us back and then we would drop into a bottomless chasm until the plane righted itself. When we finally splashed down in the Juneau harbor with water spraying up over the windows, my cells settled back into their normal places. The pilot helped me onto the dock, carried my bags to the taxi station, and told the driver to take me to the airport. Emboldened by my first flight, I felt if I could live through that, I could live through anything.

A quick change in the restroom prepared me for the rest of the journey. I teetered through the airport terminal listening to the sophisticated click of my high heels. I didn't have much of what you could call cleavage, so I wore my cowl-neck sweater backward to show off my back, which I fancied being more attractive than a flat chest. The sweater was nearly long enough to cover my bright blue pleated cheerleading skirt that came to about mid-thigh. I considered this outfit the best thing I had to make the trip. Entirely inappropriate, but I felt glam.

Once aboard the jet bound for southern California, I sank into my seat and stared out the window waiting for my new life to begin. As the powerful engines lifted us off the ground, my spirits rose with the plane and G-forces pressed me into my seat. I closed my eyes and drifted into a dreamy coma. I awoke to a prim stewardess asking me what I wanted for dinner. These were the days when a mini-pack of two cigarettes came with a full-course meal, white napkins, and wine if you were old enough. I wasn't, so I contented myself by lighting up and puffing in a most lady-like manner. Mata Hari had nothing on me as a blue haze coiled about my head and shoulders. I had smoked Camels (pilfered from my father's bureau) with my brother in his bedroom, but never in public. My first travel adventure was turning into a heady affair!

By the time I arrived in San Diego, I had changed planes successfully, struck up stirring conversations with my seatmates, gotten used to being waited on, and considered myself quite worldly. I was in no hurry to go to Grandma Fry's. Since I lived in San Diego before going to Alaska a year ago, I had connections. Instead of checking in with Grandma Fry, I called my old girlfriend Slinky Sue. Susan and I went way back. She helped me water the horses at the barn next to my house. We raced on our bikes, moving hoses from one bucket to the next. We had it down to precision timing. I hadn't seen her since my family had rudely uprooted me and taken me away from my childhood friends.

Susan came from a well-to-do family with a big house. I knew they had room for me. Her mother agreed to come and get me at the airport but was not keen on my hanging around. After a couple of days, I called Grandma Fry. She was hopping mad. It seems she had placed an all-points bulletin on me, had been praying hard, and was worried sick. This didn't start our new relationship too well, but we both knew this arrangement was temporary. We just didn't know how long temporary was going to be.

When I went back to my old school, things changed. Girlfriends squealing like pigs over some teen idol on TV at pajama parties seemed silly. They hadn't known the mature love of an 18-year-old like my Bobby. This set me apart and caused me to turn to literature for more enlightened friends. Like many readers, I began to write. It helped maintain my mental equilibrium. Paul Theroux says that "if we were normal balanced individuals, we would not write books." My disjointed childhood put me well on my way to a topsy-turvy state of mind—perfect for writing.

I loved Grandma Fry, but she had a habit of taking her false teeth out and dropping them into a glass of water on the table in the middle of a meal, which was quite off-putting. We went to church three times a week. I agreed to be baptized to get the Christians to stop praying for my lost soul and to ensure that I would not burn in hell for any past or future sins. I pined for Bobby during my absence, sending him many impassioned letters. After a year in exile, I was allowed to come home.

When I returned to Haines, Bobby and I made plans to hide behind the rows of logs piled on the dock for one last clandestine meeting. After a final feverish groping, we agreed that to avoid me being punished again, we would not see each other. I became an even more ardent reader and for solace turned to long, lonely walks along misty shores and into the dripping rainforest of southeast Alaska.

On these walks, I tried to absorb the spirit of Hootz the bear. Not that I wanted to meet him in person, but according to Tlingit lore he is the closest of all animals to humans. Plainly out of sorts with my own kind, I imagined a kinship with him. According to the legend of the woman who married a bear, "After you take a bear's coat off, it looks just like a human. And they act human: they fool, they are rowdy and curious, and they remember. They are confident. They make love for hours. They are grumpy after naps. They seem to be indestructible. They know what's happening, where to go, and how to get there. They are forgiving. They have no enemies, no fears, they can be silly, and they are big-hearted. They are completely at home in the world." To have the essence of bear in my heart would be good.

Edward Abbey, of *Desert Solitaire* fame, concluded that solitude is a brooding meditation on open spaces. My solitary youth allowed me to sink deeper into the present and internalize my impress-ions. It gave them time to settle into my mind and become a part of me. The quietude was uninterrupted by the constant awareness of a companion's comprehension of events, and the feeling that I must be entertaining in my conversation was absent. In short, I became more comfortable and in tune with the place I was in than with the people who lived there. In adult life, this quality has helped me breathe deeply into other land-scapes and to bring them to life for others in travel articles.

According to Don George, author of *Travel Writing*, the quintessential qualities of a travel writer are as follows:

"You have to be able to drop everything and take off to far-flung places at a moment's notice." I believe my first flight was perfect training for the job. "You also need to leave room for the unexpected to happen." Surely this lesson was learned. "You must be adaptable, that is, equally at home on the high seas as on the low road." I think I rose to the occasion admirably. "You will have to manage strained relationships due to long absences." Bobby did have to learn to live without me and me without him. "You must have 'pluck'. That is, you have to find the courage to talk to people you've never met, and to learn to trust in the kindness of strangers." The pilot whom I had never met before was just the first in a long list of assists from total strangers in my life. George concludes that travel writing is essentially a lonely profession. "You must possess a passion for exploring and integrating your discoveries into precise palpable prose to offset this negative." I feel fully alive when I am engaged in the state of exploration. As for palpable, as opposed to purple prose, that is something I will be working on for the rest of my life.

It seems I was handed all the ingredients to become an accomplished travel writer on my first flight. Collecting and collating data is a habit I've acquired because I like to get to a source quickly. Research is fun. Travel enlivening. Writing expands and excites my universe. Was I happy at the time about the trip that engendered personality quirks that led me to this profession? No. Am I happy about it now? You bet. The ugliest of ducklings emerged as an elegant black swan with a bright red beak and crimson feet flying high with an eclectic flock of other exotic birds.

Taking a Cue from the Que Station

January 2020 was a brilliant day in Sydney Harbor when I boarded the ferry headed for Manly headlands. I ran upstairs to the front deck to face the wind and sucked in the intoxicating air. The boat picked up speed as we left the bustle of the quay behind. Soon we were scooting past the sails of the Sydney Opera House flashing in the sun. We were off to explore the Que Station, aka the Quarantine Station, twenty minutes away. I was not certain why the Station was on the Overseas Adventure travel itinerary but was game to explore.

Our vessel stopped at the dock jutting out from an idyllic cove with a white sand swimming beach fringed by trees. A few lucky swimmers were paddling around in the turquoise waters. I felt annoyed at not being told to bring a swimsuit on this venture on such a glorious day.

Apparently, after WWI all ships entering the harbor were stopped at Manly before they were allowed to enter Sydney. The Spanish Influenza pandemic was in full swing, and all passengers were required to disembark there for decontamination. The ship owners had to pay all expenses incurred for this factory for processing people. Third-class passengers were given tents and rations and told to camp on the beach. First and second-class passengers enjoyed more luxurious accommodations, but all had to go through three cleansing steps regardless of their status.

The first stop for passengers was a stifling, windowless cubicle that our guide informed us was a gas inhalation chamber. Steam infused with zinc sulfate designed to dry out the lungs of those with the virus was flushed into the room crammed with 30-40 people. This procedure turned out to be carcinogenic and served to spread the virus rather than cure it. I felt claustrophobic in this room and couldn't wait to move on.

The next step was the "Bakers Oven." Baggage was placed on a track that moved it through a decontamination process intended to eradicate any vermin. Steam at 112 degrees mixed with formaldehyde gas did kill bugs or vermin, but it shrank the clothing a couple sizes and destroyed photos in the process. If losing your wardrobe was not enough, the third step was even more shocking.

We entered a room with rows of showers in cubbyholes. Passengers were then required to remove all their clothing and drench themselves in hot water laced with carbolic acid. This ghastly room brought visions of concentration camps to mind. Now, I wanted to run but there was nowhere to hide on this tour. The unfortunate passengers were trapped here for two weeks, until they either had no symptoms or died. The Que Station was fenced, and a long swim to Sydney.

The fourth stop on the tour was the infirmary where most people who entered never left. Figures range from 17 to 50 million people who died in the 15 months it took for the Spanish Flu to run its course worldwide. Few doctors volunteered for this deadly duty. Fifty-seven nurses, of which 27 were volunteers, were tending to the ill in 1917. Many of them died serving their patients.

The last stop was the morgue. Autopsies were performed and organs of the deceased were harvested for research in hopes of finding a cure.

All the while I was on the tour, I kept asking myself what has this to do with me? I live in the modern age where vaccines and cures are available to prevent and stop diseases. When I returned to the U.S. in February the coronavirus pandemic was raging in China. By March, Los Angeles, where I live, was shut down. The streets of downtown L.A. were empty, the skyscrapers shuttered, and the air was the cleanest it's been in my lifetime. How could this be happening? Our scientists can conquer anything! Right? We were told to shelter in place and wear a mask when we left home. Hardly the intensity of the diabolic measures taken to combat the Spanish flu, the black plague, smallpox, and other horrific pandemics. This seems a small price to pay to head the Covid 19 virus off at the pass. Six months into the pandemic we are no closer to containment and the travel industry is in tatters.

Ironically, the Que Station (which has not been in operation for many) years offers lodging at an affordable price in the housing that was built for upper-class passengers. You can watch the sailboats ply Sydney Harbor, swim in a sweet little cove, and enjoy self-quarantine before entering society. I wish we had that option here in the U.S. for those venturing out in the world who don't want to chance infecting loved ones when they return home. A fully sanitized facility with room service and a pool for exercise near major transport hubs would be a welcome option for this travel writer.

Lost Angel Gets Cold Wings

From my tiny capsule chugging through space, I overlook the 20 million acres of the largest protected region crossing international borders on Earth. The heart-thumping ride in a small plane from Glacier Bay to Haines, Alaska over the St. Elias range is described as a "short scenic flight" in the guidebooks. Snow-frosted spires stacked to infinity fan out in celestial whiteness. Below, the Lynn Canal, a sun-spangled mirror of water, is streaked with the triangle tails of tiny fishing boats. Sitka spruce forest blankets valleys carved by sparkling rivers. I'm glad to witness terrain so remote, rugged, and treacherous that no earthmover would dare to approach it, but I feel anxious. My palms are clammy, and I can't stop rubbing my thighs.

We fly close to the barren peaks that support no visible life. They are copper colored, not black as they appear when looking at them from the distant ground. The granite saddles with patches of snow look like giant sleeping brown cows mottled with white. I spy a moose marsh, a happy spot for beaver, martin, and more.

"Wings" is considered one of the safest, best-maintained small airlines servicing southeast Alaska, but I can't help listening for a sputter in the engine. I examine the back of the pilot's head and wonder what he did the night before. Did he get a good rest? Was he recovering from a bender? His bushy red hair gave no clue.

Jennifer, a ground scout for a major cruise line, and her female companion are the only other passengers. She is an experienced skydiver and holds no fear of turbulence. When the pilot announces, "It's going to get bumpy," she offers me her hand. I gratefully take the hand of a stranger, knowing that if the plane goes down, we may share eternity. I feel blessed to have her at my side and try to absorb her calm.

"I have jumped out of planes this size hundreds of times," she says laughing. Her lightheartedness gives me courage when the tiny plane starts to bounce like a rubber ducky in a perfect storm. Jennifer's friend, sitting in the co-pilot seat, is blowing bubbles and smacking her gum furiously. She is listening to heavy metal from the headset provided by the pilot. Jennifer offers me a headset. I refuse. I don't want to be distracted from my own demise.

Just before leaving L. A. to visit my family in Haines, I saw a two-inch article describing an accident on a flight over this very glacier field. All six passengers and the pilot died instantly when their plane slammed into a mountain.

"What happened on the flight that crashed?" I yelled to the pilot over the din of the engine.

"The pilot tipped the wing so the group could get a better look at a couple bears. They were too low to the ground when he dipped. He couldn't recover in time. That's why they call it "Look a Bear Air." He laughed just before banking hard to the left so we could get a better view of Davidson Glacier.

The river of ice, mud, and rock below looks like whipped marble cake batter. When it reaches a ledge hundreds of feet above the canal, the hanging glacier transforms itself into an aquamarine waterfall that plunges into the jade green water of the canal. Not even the splendor of this crystal creation can take my mind off impending doom. I promise my Maker that I will write letters of thanks to everyone I've meant to in this lifetime if I am granted another day.

A tiny landing strip appears in the distance. Inwardly I vow that when my toes touch terra firma, I will never leave the ground again in anything smaller than a 747. In moments the pilot makes a masterful landing. I feel my molecules settling back into place. Jennifer hops to the ground and turns to help me out. She gives me a huge hug. I feel her strength flow through me. My eyes glisten with tears as I watch her skip off to her next "short scenic flight" over the St. Elias range to Skagway. I envy her boundless bravery. "Namaste," I say and wave goodbye. On the shuttle into town, I add Jennifer to my growing list of friends who will receive a letter of gratitude from me out of the blue.

The Best of Times
with Bobo in Taylor Camp

While living on the north shore of Kauai in the '70s, I got a job as a cub reporter at the *Kauai Garden Island News*. This gave me access to people on the Island I found noteworthy. Suzanne "Bobo" Bollins, who lived at the notorious Taylor Camp (1969-1977) where young people fleeing the Vietnam War and materialism of the mainland were living out the ultimate hippie fantasies, seemed a good prospect. It was said that Bobo swam the tumultuous waters of the Napali Coast wearing only a belt with a pouch containing food for when she reached the shore. This seemed quite a miraculous feat to me, so I made an appointment to interview her.

Bobo was known to be a heavy drinker. I heard she had been locked in the trunk of a police car until she calmed down. People were accustomed to her creating a disturbance when she had too much to drink. She welcomed me in her tree house abode with a tumbler of Merlot. She seemed perfectly at ease in her Spartan quarters, forerunner to the tiny house movement today. Her brown skin was weathered from the sun and a thick braid of golden hair went to her waist. Stories of the residents cavorting nude were over-stated, she told me. She was wearing a sarong tied at the shoulder in the early Hawaiian kikepa style, and said regular clothes were worn by residents in the evenings to fend off mosquitoes.

"When did you arrive in Taylor Camp?" I asked.

"I was one of the first to call it home. I was busted on the mainland for marijuana and the authorities were going to take my two daughters away from me. So, when I heard about the camp, I came straight away."

"So, you brought your daughters with you?"

"Yes, I couldn't bear them being placed in a foster home. My marriage was broken… I knew I couldn't fix myself fast enough. I believe they are better off living a free life here with me than with a stranger."

"Are they happy here?"

"Yes. Alpin, my youngest, is happy to have a permanent home. She wants to be "normal." Minka is a water baby like me. She spends her days surfing and playing in the tide pools with the other kids."

"I am fascinated by your desire to swim the Napali Coast. What is it like to be in some of the most treacherous waters in Hawai'i for so many hours?"

"It is like a meditation. I swim in the nude. I

24

swim face down wearing snorkel, mask, and fins. I grease up my body with wheat germ oil to protect me from the sun and it helps keep me warm. My arms, legs, and breath find their rhythm and my body goes onto automatic pilot. It is like an out-of-body experience where I am no longer in charge of what is happening. The currents and wind are mostly in my favor swimming down the Napali Coast. It is kind of like being a bird gliding on thermals. When I go all the way to Polahali, another five miles from Kalalau, I take a sarong with me. I have to hitch a ride around the Island to get back to Taylor Camp where I can ditch my clothes again."

The state of consciousness she described was one I had read that many long-distance swimmers experience.

"Aren't you afraid sharks?"

"When I see a big fish it jolts me back into my body, but they have never bothered me."

Dolphin often played with her on her swims from Ke'e Beach to Kalalau Valley, some six miles away. Their intelligence was evident when they came close to look her in the eye. They would swim with her for miles shooting back and forth inviting her to play. "It is uplifting and joyous to be with them." She was highly animated in the telling of her month-long stays in the Kalalau Valley which is held sacred by Hawaiians.

"The valley is closed off from the rest of the

world at the end of the Kalalau trail. It is steeped in mana (spiritual energy). The vibes are intense. Kauai is the oldest of the Hawaiian Islands. Locals say there is a mantle of mana protecting the Island from invasions. Kalalau is my healing place. It is where I escape from everything I can't change."

"What makes you want to do these dangerous long-distance swims alone?"

"My swims are what saves me from myself. Sometimes, I feel like there is a cold wind blowing through my heart. I try to drink and drug it away, but that never really works. If it weren't for my swims, I would likely be dead from alcoholism."

Our conversation stopped abruptly when she announced that the lava rocks in the canvas-domed sauna just below her treehouse were ready. This was to be an evening of sharing with the other residents in the camp. Bobo offered me a hit off a joint of the most powerful pot I have ever run into.

"Would you like to join us in a ceremony celebrating Earth Mother?" she asked.

Curious minds want to know, so I stripped to my undies and joined the group wearing no more than their birthday suits. We sat in a circle around the steaming crimson rocks holding hands while chant-ing a reverberating OM. The heat generated by the cauldron of molten lava rocks combined with the intense communal sharing of energy brought me to a feverish crescendo. I stumbled out of the sauna and planted myself face down in the frigid mountain stream running through the camp to cool off. Energy shot through the top of my head like a comet, leaving my mind as clear as the sparkling heavens above.

At that time, the highly romanticized camp of peace and love hippies, glorified in coffee table books today, was nearing an end. Elizabeth Taylor's brother, Howard, who owned seven acres of beach-front property had originally allowed a group of thirteen disenfranchised youth from San Francisco to build their camp on Ke'e Beach. Soon, there were over 120 people, including women with small children living at the camp. The residents of Taylor Camp who did not pay taxes and lived on welfare and food stamps, soon found themselves at odds with the locals. Further, native Hawaiians didn't like the desecration taking place in the Kalalau Valley. It was rumored that home boys had put a dead pig upstream the week before my visit to contaminate the water and encourage the treehouse people to move on.

Still, I admired Bobo for her extreme bravery and athleticism. At the time I did not know that I had found the inspiration for the dolphin that would be the loyal friend of my heroine in *Wai-nani, A Voice from Old Hawai'i*. It is fascinating to witness how life experiences boomerang into an artist's consciousness and appear in their work. Many *Wai-nani* readers view her relationship with a dolphin family as fantastic. The truth is that all the interaction between my heroine and her best friend Eku, a bottlenose dolphin, is real. That is to say, I researched the behavior of dolphins and their relationship with humans throughout history to bring authenticity to the story. A two-part documentary film directed by Robert C. Stone detailing life in Taylor Camp was released in the Islands in 2009. (It is available on Youtube.com). Bobo's granddaughter, Natalie Noble, stars in the film re-enacting Bobo swimming alone in the buff along the majestic Napali Coast. I suspect there are dolphins playing in her wake.

Note: Some of Bobo's responses to my questions are taken from Robert C. Stone's film.

Let Me Go for You

While I was entertained by hideous reptiles resting on the shoulders of boys at the beach in Puerta Vallarta, my mother, a frisky 70-year-old, was fascinated with people parasailing ten stories high over the bay. Drawn like a cobra to a flute, she got up and headed for the motorboat that took the more daring aloft. I ran after her and talked her into letting me go for her this time.

Before I knew it, I was strapped in a frayed nylon harness heading skyward with my stomach dropping to my toes. As I scanned the panoramic coastline, I realized I was higher than any of the hotels lining the shore. I saw my body suspended at the end of a rope tether tended by three small brown men in a speedboat. The full horror of my predicament set in when I hit an air pocket. My precarious nylon seat dropped twenty feet in a second. After several giddy minutes, the boys positioned me above the sandy beach and slowed the engine so the parachute would drop me down slowly. I was supposed to run upon impact. Instead, I hit hard and crumpled up like a broken beach umbrella. I limped back to our beach towel to make my report.

"You could break a hip on landing. I really don't think you should go up," I said. My mother glowered into the sand like a petulant child. For the rest of our stay, she was sullen.

One year later, she wrangled a trip to Hawaii with a group of fellow seniors. There she was lifted into the air from the water by a speedboat and won the admiration of her peers for her parasailing technique. I had stood in her way in Mexico, she scrawled on a palm tree-studded postcard. My act of heroism had robbed her of her independence.

I vowed that in the future I would save life-threatening, random acts of insanity for my own calls to adventure.

Jack London and Me

Trotting behind my guide along the trails that Jack London once rode, I imagined myself as one of the many friends he led on horseback rides through his 1,400 acre Beauty Ranch in the early 1900's. We galloped through stands of eucalyptus, madrone, and towering redwoods shading the fern-filled glens that were just as Jack described them in his novel The Valley of the Moon. Delighted with each new vista, I too felt "vitalized, organic" as I overlooked the vineyards in neat, tidy rows stretching to the foot of the purple Sonoma Mountains. We cantered over a rise to see the lake that Jack and Charmian, his wife of eleven years, swam in on sunny afternoons. I saw myself gliding with them through the clear water and drying on a hot rock in the sun, cooled by the wisp of a breeze.

Like young Jack London, I went from California to the Northwest while in my teens. Unlike Jack, it was not my idea of a great adventure. My parents, determined to homestead in Haines, Alaska, rudely uprooted me and took me to a world populated by loggers, fishermen, and Tlingit Indians. At thirteen, I hadn't read Jack's White Fang or The Call of the Wild. I didn't know I was walking in the famous author's footsteps when I took the narrow-gauge train that snakes up the Whitehorse Pass into the Yukon. I had no idea it was the alternate route for the Chilkoot Trail Jack climbed, carrying a 150-pound pack, during the Gold Rush of the 1890s.

A decade after my family's shift to the north, Hollywood chose to use the more accessible Dalton Trail from Haines to the Klondike to re-enact the fabled climb of the stampeders up the ice steps of the Chilkoot Trail in the movie White Fang. Every able-bodied person in my hometown was hired to recreate the famous scene Jack described. Even then, while everyone in town swaggered about bragging about his or her role in the film, I still had no personal aware-ness of Jack London. He was simply an adventurer who captured the grit of the northwest in "children's books."

It was not until my own personal call to adven-ture took me to Hawaii that I tasted the vitality of Jack's writing. I found solace in the gentle beauty of the Islands and envied the athletic bodies of the Hawaiians and their connection with the sea and nature. While living on Kauai, I came to respect and admire their culture and began to delve into the history of old Hawaii. It was here that the seed for my historical novel, Wai-nani: A Voice from Old Hawai'i, took root. In my research, I was pleasantly surprised to find Jack London's Hawaiian stories.

Jack London made the "blue water crossing" to the Territory of Hawaii in 1907 from San Francisco on the barely seaworthy Snark. "The Sailor on Horseback "sailed for two years throughout the South Seas collecting adventures for his stories. Over a period of thirteen years, he returned many times to Hawaii, his favorite resting spot. He showed great aloha (love) for the Islands and loved to hear the stories of the Kanaka and delved deep into the myths of old Hawaii handed down in the chants of elders. While writing my fictionalized account of the life of Ka'ahumanu, the favorite wife of Kamehameha the Great, I read Jack's Hawaii stories for inspiration and insight into the minds of the ancients. I studied the techniques used by the master of engaging writing and prayed that what I absorbed would filter through my own writing.

After roaming the globe Jack came home to his Beauty Ranch where he died at age forty from uremic poisoning. After my ride, I sought out his simple gravesite surrounded by a weathered wooden fence. By this time, I had read all of Jack's major works and couple of books written about him. I felt a spiritual connection with a man who died a century ago. It seemed he had been with me all my life; forging ahead of me, sharing his insights, giving me guidance from the grave. For me there was no time between us. The man who religiously wrote a thousand words a day departed in silence. No one spoke at his service, as though there were no more words left to say.

Years after my visit to Beauty Ranch, I found the memory of Jack London again at the Huntington Hartford Museum in Pasadena. I was drawn to a collection of letters written in his hand. "Writing is about action, struggle, conflict and resolution," he said. Jack spent many hours reading the work of novices, editing their pieces and giving words of encouragement. My tears streamed as turbulent emotions rose from deep inside. Writing, often a thankless and unnoticed endeavor, had great urgency for me once more. I wanted to thank Jack London for his kindness and generosity of spirit. Though I don't possess the fire to blast through life like a superb meteor as Jack London did, I do strive to write consistently. I try not to be afraid to write about what is important to me and to be honest with my readers. I look to him for strength on those days when my soul cries tired.

A Symphony in the Key of Green

The fortune cookie at my farewell dinner in Los Angeles promised *You will have many friends when you need them.*

Pinned to a rock ledge, watching the lowering sun glint off the headwaters of New Zealand's Hukere Stream above me, I hoped one of those friends would soon appear. The rest of the trampers in South Island's Nelson Lakes National Forest had already congregated for the evening at Angelus Hut, the hub of a spiral of tracks throughout this less-traveled region of the Southern Alps in New Zealand. An enforced rest gave me time to reflect upon why I had come to gaze upon the sparkling streams of water fanning across the rock walls on the far side of the chasm I was facing.

It all started about seven years ago when I was laying low with your garden variety L4-L5 herniated disc. Unwilling to trust a scalpel-wielding surgeon any-where near my spinal cord, I embarked on a path of self-healing. Finding solace in Mother Nature's handi-work, I became absorbed in the meditative state that comes with putting one foot in front of another on long walks through the mountains. The silver lining to my crisis was that as my back got better, I became a fit hiker.

I read about the hut-to-hut trekking adventures on the hundreds of miles of tracks that lace through New Zealand. Images of alpine meadows and frothy waterfalls tumbling down craggy spires through primordial rainforests called to me like a siren's song. I chose Active New Zealand, one of two commercial outfitters with permits to use the Department of Conservation huts on a three-day tramp from St. Arnaud. This track with a 3,500-elevation gain runs along the eastern shore of Lake Rotoiti to Lake Head, across the Travers River, and up the Cascade Track to Angelus Hut.

My Kiwi guide, Kyle, collected me and the other five members of the group in Christchurch, the largest city on the South Island. Our van plunged over hill and valley snaking over the two-lane highway proudly hailed as Number One. "We don't need any more roads," Kyle yelled over his shoulder. "With only 850,000 people living here year-round, what's the point? Besides, we like the green, not concrete."

We blasted down a windswept coast passing through gray clouds hovering over green pastures on our way to Kaikoura. A good night's rest and a full breakfast later, we headed into the bush. The shakedown walk along the shores of Lake Rotoiti into Lake Head Hut, taught me that my tricky back couldn't handle the weight of my pack. The other guests on the trip let me stash my clothing in their packs. Gordon, a 26-year-old telecommunications wizard, got my fleece pants and sweater. Jeff, a 29-year-old, chivalrous Canadian, took my sleeping bag, and Lutz, a stocky ex-soccer player, got to be my camera caddy. Gretchen, the only other woman on the trip, carried her pack without a whimper. Her husband Dean, blessed with bionic energy, picked up the slack by carrying our group's kitchen gear.

Spirits soared when we headed out through a meadow of golden tussocks spiked with purple bells suspended from tall stalks. Jeff offered me his hand when we waded through the frigid, knee-high rush of the Travers River. This unavoidable crossing at the onset of the march keeps lightweights off this track. Lutz, another mature hiker from California, lent me one of his hiking sticks so that I could navigate the root-strewn trail up the mountain and hop boulders in the many creek crossings along the way. The twenty-somethings sprang up the trail like deer and were soon out of sight.

Lutz and I fell into the same category of being in good shape for our age, but not as fit as the average outdoor-loving Kiwi. As we followed the little red triangles hammered onto the trees, I felt like a child chasing after witches' crumbs deep into the gloom of the silver and red beech forests. White clematis twined about the twisted limbs of aging trees. Three-quarters of the amazing variety of plants growing here are endemic, with over eighty species of fern alone, but I was struck by the lack of blooming plants.

Unlike other subtropical climes I have visited, there was no profusion of fragrant, bright-colored flowers. Even though the foliage had the look of a tropical jungle, the air was crisp, almost alpine. It was a splendid blend that kept me energized as I marched ever upward through the cool spreading fronds of fern, thick layers of moss lichens, and epiphytic vines that converged to create a symphony in the key of green.

The friendly gossip of the energetic Hukere Stream churning over black boulders kept us company as it paralleled the challenging climb to Angelus Hut. From the cool depths, I heard the liquid voice of the bellbird and the eerie call of the New Zealand pigeon.

Kyle, a 6-foot 5-inch, 250-pound, civilized silverback gorilla kind of a guy, stayed a few steps behind us ensuring that we didn't stray. He offered a hand up rocky ledges and shared secrets of the flora and fauna when we took a break. His father is a Māori chief, and his mother is a Pakeha (white New Zealander). He has consciously taken the best of both cultures into his heart. He unfurled the frond of a fiddle fern for us to examine.

"The tendrils of the mother fern hide thousands of fern pods that the Māori people see as children of the forest," he explained.

"Soon these pods will propagate and rejuvenate the rain forest with new life."

Listening to him tell the stories of the Polynesian people who came here in hundred-foot canoes about 1,200 AD changed my point of view. The swirling patterns tattooed upon their face and bodies that made them look fierce were simply imitations of the lush, life-giving forest around them.

Birds like tomtits, robins, tiny rifleman, and the flashy fantail twittered from the tree canopy. Kyle told us he receives messages from the fantail when sad things happen in his family. New Zealand's national bird, the black tui, with a flashy white ball at his throat, is the most common and raucous songster of the forest. I listened to his chortles as we continued up the soggy trail with mist rising from the damp under-story heated by the sun streaming through giant tree ferns.

When the cool glades of the forest opened to a sun-drenched meadow, we were surrounded by an amphitheater of snow-crowned peaks jutting into end-less blue skies. An exhausted Lutz took a snooze in the sun while I meditated upon the three-tiered water-fall cascading from the summit a thousand feet above us.

After lunch, we crossed the river at the base of the waterfall and began the last climb. Water oozed through the rock crevices. I stepped carefully into the footsteps of those who had gone before. The ascent became a steep hand-over-hand effort. My pack, even though significantly lighter, threatened to pull me off balance. Looking down upon the growing chasm, I feared I'd taken on more than I could handle. Could my injured back withstand the rigors of the climb? If I became crippled while backpacking in New Zealand there would be little sympathy for me at home. Lun-acy is not held in great esteem where I come from.

Thirteen miles into the hike I was too weak to take one more step up or down. I looked around for Lutz and Kyle who had apparently fallen into a hobbit hole. Easing onto the rock ledge, I sucked in the scintillating air and let my body go limp using my backpack for an easy chair. The sun warmed the tension from my shoulders. The expression deliriously happy took on new meaning. I'd liked to have stayed there forever, but I knew that when the sun slipped behind the lip of the summit the temperature would plummet and the frosty heavens sparkling with a billion stars would be no comfort especially since my fleeces were tucked into Gordon's pack.

"Hallo down there," ricocheted off the rock walls surrounding me.

Kyle suddenly appeared on the ledge above me. He and Lutz had taken a different route and were almost to the top. He bounded down the steep cliff face like a sure-footed mountain goat.

"Would you like some help?" he asked with a broad grin. Extending a strong, muscled arm, he lifted me up onto the ledge where he stood.

"How far is it?" I asked, afraid of the answer.

"No worries. You're almost there."

I relinquished my backpack to him and clambered up the last hundred yards to Angelus Hut, which sits beside a glittering alpine lake in the hollow of a glacier cirque. My group, along with an international array of backpackers, was sprawled on wooden decks soaking up the last rays of the sun when I arrived.

Kyle whipped up a pasta dish that made the

trekkers eating food from freeze-dried packets warmed over Bunsen burners envious. It's an odd sensation to settle down for the night on communal bunks with strangers. But at the end of a hiking day, everyone "snugs down" into their sleeping bags, leaving decorum behind. The cacophony of snores betrays no accent.

I rose early with the rest to catch the blush of the morning sun. The hike out across Robert's Ridge involved a scramble up a steep face followed by boulder hopping on a goat trail to get to an easy romp across the top of the world. Lutz and I took our time to admire the outrageous vistas of serrated peaks and the green patchwork quilt of farms far below. Rare alpine vegetation included sage-green barrels with white flowers, yellow clumps of mat daisy, and blue mounds of what are called vegetable sheep. A late afternoon switchback through flower fields on a south-facing slope overlooking jade-green Rotoroa Lake ended our trek.

Kyle was waiting for us beside the lake with a chest full of cold beer. As I cooled my blistered dogs in the icy water, triumphant tears welled. The hike was daunting, but with the help of a few strong friends, I had shattered the glass house of physical restriction that I feared was mine forever. Fortune cookies and other fairy tales can come true.

Rafting in the Wake of
Georgie White - Woman of the River

*I love it above everything. I have often listened to it,
gazed at it, and I have always learned something
from it.
One can learn much from a river.*
–Siddhartha-Herman Hesse

"Wake up people! Find your behind and sit on it," Captain Adam yelled over the roar of the monster wave spilling into a 20-foot hole dead ahead.

"It's the biggest water I've seen here," he said as he motored ever closer to Lava Falls. The flips at this very place—the most fearsome rapids on the 227-mile Grand Canyon run—were notorious. I bolted from my daydreaming position on the warm pontoon. While drifting between walls of porous black rock once inside the cone of a volcano, I'd sunk into river time. Ominous walls scoured by bubbling lava from the molten core of the earth held me spellbound. When we floated past the enormous basalt plug in the middle of the river, I'd forgotten that it meant we were approaching Lava Falls and that I was holding a one-way ticket home.

The enormous wave cascading over the lip of the rock was begging to catch a boatman in a mistake. We planned to stay to the right of the hole to avoid being swallowed by the river. I could see water spitting from the churning brew as we headed for the maelstrom. I held onto the straps for all I was worth and prayed I wouldn't get washed off the raft. My mantra on this trip was "stay on the boat!" A thrashing bull ride later, it was over leaving us clapping and laughing as we rocked and rolled through the rest of the wave train.

When Georgie White ran Lava Falls before the

installation of Glen Canyon Dam in 1964, the volume of water was often five times what we experienced. Upsets were the norm, and many rafters swam for their life. In 1869 when John Wesley Powell led the first recorded run of the Grand Canyon, he portaged supplies and had his men line their wooden boats downstream past Lava Falls. In the 1940s, Georgie not only rafted the entire run through the canyon solo twenty times, but she also swam through the 100+ rapids on the run in a life vest. The "Woman of the River" as she liked to call herself, admitted that the rapids were her first love. "Truthfully, there is nothing in life as exciting as shooting a wild, surging rapid," she said. But the peace she felt in the Grand Canyon when she rafted the entire 280 miles in 21 days without seeing another human being called her back repeatedly. The continuum of nature counter-balanced her life of selling real estate in Los Angeles in the winter. She ran the canyon over one hundred times before she decided it was her mission to share the canyon with others.

When she first began the campaign to bring people to the Grand Canyon, they thought she was deranged. She turned into a one-woman PR firm going on talk shows and courting Hollywood film-makers to come to the river. Today, she might be sorry she created such enthusiasm for white water rafting. May through September, the river corridor is populated with river rats in wooden dories, small paddle boats, oar boats, and motorized launches that carry 14 passengers and two guides like the one I was on. The National Park Service had to place a limit of 20,000 people on the river each year to preserve the wilderness experience for all.

The 37-foot raft with pontoons on each side used by Grand Canyon Expeditions is steered by a guide at the motor arm of an outboard. It's called a G-rig named after Georgie. She was the first to strap three Salvation Army rafts together to create a craft buoyant enough to handle everything the river had to offer. It allowed anyone with a spirit of adventure to take this journey through deep time. Whatever discomfort involved with camping out for a week and living amid mercurial weather patterns that made no apology for changing on a whim are forgotten in the rush of the rapids. Ever-widening panoramas of cathedral buttes, terracotta terraces marbled with veins of quartz, and Vishnu Schist must be experienced firsthand. No one leaves this canyon unmoved by its sheer scope.

At Lee's Ferry, fifteen miles below Glen Canyon Dam (the take-out point for the trip), the river is aquamarine and stocked with trout. When Georgie ran the river before the installation of the dam, the river ran red from sediments and warmed to 70 degrees in the summer. Today the water released from the bottom of the dam is a chilly 55 degrees requiring travelers to wear rain suits that Georgie would have found silly.

Before she rafted the river, Georgie White hiked the many trails lacing the canyon walls with her friend Harry Aleson. Harry asked her if she ever got tired or felt any pain from demanding scrambles over treacherous shale. She replied that she was numb to life since the tragic death of her 15-year-old daughter, Sommona Rose, who had been killed by a hit-and-run driver. After two years of this grueling distraction from her sorrow, she found solace in the canyon. Its only constant, change, satisfied her restless spirit.

When she started commercial runs in the '50s, she always took her guests on the steep hike up to the granaries carved into the cliffs by the Puebloan people in 1100 AD at Nankoweap. We camped on the delta below and made the same stair-stepper climb. The storage rooms for corn grown by the native people are impressive, but the sweeping vista of the pumpkin coliseum cupping the coffee-brown Colorado wending its way to the Gulf of Mexico is mystical. At dusk, the setting sun warms the canyon walls to a rosy glow as though shining through a stained-glass window.

Deer Creek, a blaze of white water cascading 100 feet out of polished red rock, has carved a sinuous gorge that can only be explored on foot. The stiff climb up to a flat rock ledge tracing this deep cleft in the canyon opens to an Eden-like paradise shaded by emerald green cottonwood trees. The Paiutes hold this site high as it is the jumping-off place for spirits into the afterlife. Hoops were placed in their ears so that when their spirits made the crossing, they could be caught by the ancestors waiting for them on the other side. The soft chatter of Deer Creek that continues to sculpt the snaking sandstone gorge is all that is heard in this sacred chamber.

Georgie was happy with a tin of tomatoes in her backpack for sustenance. She found that a vegetarian diet gave her boundless energy. Contrary to her Spartan ways, we enjoyed meals of grilled halibut, chicken, and tender filet mignon with a variety of wholesome salads and side dishes. Every night Captain Adam and Chelsea, his assistant guide, served us cake warm from a Dutch oven. Breakfasts were blueberry muffins, French toast, yogurt, egg sandwiches, fruit, cereals, sausages, and more. I've thought about changing my carnivore ways, but it wouldn't be on this trip!

Days on the river seem to collide with one another. Some people wore watches, but I couldn't understand why. We chatted in the cool mornings over coffee with the smell of crisping bacon in the air while the sun peeked over the rim illuminating the canyon walls that protected us from any news from outside. Now part of the natural rhythms of the canyon, we awoke at first light and were in bed when the sun dipped down behind the rim after a full day of rafting and hiking. I slept under blinking stars and loved gazing up at the Big Dipper with a light warm breeze on my cheek and no mosquitoes to ruin the spell. The only flying insects were gnats that were dinner for the hundreds of bats that flickered between me and a brilliant full moon.

I envied Georgie her time alone here. Her words rang in my ears. "Once you enter the world of that canyon on the Colorado River you are alone. I mean, completely alone. There were many times during those first years that I would run the entire 280 miles from Lee's Ferry to Lake Mead without seeing another soul. Imagine, if you can, the state of being completely cut off and unable to speak to another person for two to three weeks at a time."

I could imagine. And I did have a few moments to myself at Stone Canyon where a bubbling flow tumbles over a rim of a red rock framed in maidenhair ferns and green mosses. My skin was dry from the alkaline-rich waters of the Little Colorado where we had giggled down a water slide earlier that day. I tore off my clothes and stood under the tingling spray that made me think about the power of water. The element that in six million years sculpted this canyon a mile below the rim of the Colorado Plateau, unearthing basement rock that is 1.7 billion years old, is the same element that gives life to us all. I sat before this lively waterfall and gave thanks to Earth Mother.

Each day on the river brought new wonders. On Day One, we motored through serene stretches of sandstone pharaohs, sphinx, and thunderbirds. I saw Kokopeli, the randy prankster of the Southwest, who led many an Indian maid astray with his magic flute. A burst of white spewing from polished red rock called Vasey's Falls seemed a miracle after miles of arid monoliths. Upper Granite Gorge on Day Two—or was it three?—is a fun 40 miles of roller coaster rapids with big waves splashing over our bow. Where the opalescent waters of Little Colorado merge with the now murky Colorado, marks the end of Marble Canyon and the beginning of the Grand. Vistas widen, temples rise, cathedral buttes now olive green with sage-covered shoulders stippled with barrel cactus spread to the rim ten miles away. Mysterious slot canyons carved by creeks merging with the main vein beg to be explored. Caverns in the river wall streaked with black and white designs recall the pottery of the Native Americans who have long made this canyon their home. Clouds of teal-backed swallows and black and white swifts did fast flight maneuvers about our heads. Herons on the shore stand like sticks hoping to be ignored. A mountain sheep stares at us with dull recognition as we glide by his shore. It's just another day on the river and each day there is more.

I kept asking myself why it was so important for me to raft in the wake of Georgie White. Is it because

I too sell real estate in Los Angeles and need to reach for the freedom demanded by a wild spirit? Chelsea, a full-fledged boatwoman who takes guests down the river in an oar boat, told me the river was like a relative she must come back and visit each year. She needs to see how the river has changed the beaches and churned up the rapids and to feel the embrace of the canyon once more. I learned that I loved going with the flow of the strong current carrying us into unbroken time. I felt vitally alive living in the present watching for signs of what was to come—shifting clouds, rising winds, whirling eddies, sounds of rapids looming ahead. I felt a powerful jolt of electric energy while doing my meditations. It's an energy that Adam says can steal your soul. An Indian friend told Adam he must call his soul back from the river at the end of each season lest it is tempted to stay during unforgiving winters. Like the Woman of the River and all the brave women who paddle in her wake, he too is captive to the charms of the canyon.

Train's on Fire

It's late. My reading light is the only one that's on in the sleeping car. I rock with the sway of the train as it clicks through the night. The rest of the passengers are dozing. Some snore like loggers, others jerk awake and collapse back into contorted positions trying to find a comfortable way to sleep sitting up.

A tiny cone of light illuminates my book, *Man and His Symbols,* by Jung. I was curious about subconscious motivations that emerge when triggered. I was also intrigued by the idea of collective consciousness and ideas percolating up through society and how we are all united by them. Jung explains how one idea will come to the surface in society all over the world seemingly at once demonstrating how we share this commonality of consciousness through shared experiences. This seemed a logical theory to me that I have witnessed.

Suddenly, the man directly in front of me stood up, turned around, looked directly at me, and said, "Train's on fire. File out to the left."

I could see that even though his eyes were open he was in a trance—a dream-like state. I couldn't resist observing him in this condition. I could have tried to awaken him, but I wanted to watch him go through this manifestation of the powerful dream state I was reading about. I believe he was totally unaware of what he was doing.

He was about 30 with pale skin and a shock of dishwater blonde hair that stood up in a dishelmed heap on his head. His eyes were gray green. There was no center to them. There seemed to be no connection to his consciousness. It was as though he was looking back inside his head. He proceeded to go down the car waking every other person gently nudging them on the shoulder and saying, "Train's on fire. File out to the left."

Within ten minutes, pandemonium had set in the compartment. The gentleman across from me struggled to get his baggage out from the overhead bin. He pulled with such force it snapped open and his freshly pressed shirts wrapped in plastic covers slid all over the floor. He grabbed for the shirts while another section of his bag opened letting papers fly. He scrambled wildly to collect his belongings before they were trampled upon by the growing panic-stricken crowd.

A young pregnant woman with a three-year-old in tow put on her jacket, held back tears, and headed for the door. An elderly couple began pressing their way to the rear door with the old man threatening with his umbrella. Thrashing overhead he made his way through the aisle swelling with terrified people.

The lights went on. Everyone froze. All the passengers were awake when the conductor came through the front hatch of the compartment.

"Sit down! Keep quiet," he yelled.

The pregnant woman cried, "The train is on fire we have got to get out of here."

With that, the entire car full of crazed people started shoving like cattle from a brush fire. They clamored toward the exit in a crushing effort to get out.

The conductor tried to hold them back. "Sit down. Sit down. You can't get out! The train is moving. You are not going anywhere. There is no fire."

The man who had been going down the aisle waking people up came forward. He quietly walked up to the conductor and whispered, "Don't be alarmed. Train's on fire, file out to the left."

The conductor took a steady look at him, grabbed his shirt by the lapels and gave him a solid slap across the face, then shook him violently. With that, the man woke up as though being dragged from a deep sleep. Seemingly, unaware of anything that had happened, he was dazed and confused.

The conductor was furious. "If you don't shut up and go to sleep, I'm going to throw you off this train!"

The man looked around guessing he was the cause of some hideous misadventure and pleaded for mercy.

"I'm so sorry I didn't know," he said.

"Well, sorry wouldn't have been good enough if someone had got hurt tonight. Now turn your lights out and go back to sleep everyone."

The conductor sat the man back down in his seat and the people began to settle down. I continued to read late into the night. I was unnerved by this powerful display of the subconscious mind. I felt somewhat guilty for not awakening the man, but I didn't want to interfere with the drama unfolding before me. I was glad when the conductor arrived as things were out of hand.

The next morning, I saw the man in the dining car having breakfast with his companion. I asked if I could join them. They welcomed me. It turned out that he and his partner lived in Laurel Canyon, just around the corner from where I live in Studio City. The man was a schoolteacher who led a most ordinary life.

I had to ask him what prompted him to behave the way he did.

"I don't know what got into me," he said, "Nothing like this has happened before."

His partner chastised him saying, "Next time, could you just keep your death wish to yourself!"

I felt sorry for the poor man who had no control over his subconscious mind. According to Jung, our minds manifest our thoughts in dreams without our permission or repression. Our bodies are just along for the ride. Our dreams can be our best guides, but the idea that we can control them seems impossible to me.

I'm glad the train was not on fire. But I was afraid to go to sleep for fear I would reveal my deepest, darkest secrets to a carload of strangers. I didn't get a wink as we rocked and rolled through the Rocky Mountains and on to New York.

Bright Blossom of the Pacific

Oh, the life on breezy hills on countless horses.
This is the life meant for me.
All my gear and occupations on the saddle and no
thought of care.
—Isabella Bird 1873

When Isabella Bird at the age of 40 set sail for Australia and New Zealand, the Hawaiian Islands were not on her mind. Desperate for diversion from the dreary weather of Scotland and nagging maladies that kept her bedridden, she found solace in travel. She suffered from botched operations to remove carbuncles on her spine and was bled regularly with incisions and by leeches. She was so weak that doctors placed her in a steel brace to help her hold herself erect. An early victim of overdosing, she was given laudanum (opium extract) and cannabis, and was encouraged to drink copious amounts of alcohol to soothe the pain. Is it any wonder she was depressed?

A frightful storm off New Zealand blew the rickety vessel she was sailing on into Honolulu Bay for repair. This serendipitous mooring served to change Isabella's life forever. The ship was only in the harbor for a week but, beguiled by the island's beauty, Isabella went on what she termed a "ravage" of the Hawaiian Islands that lasted over six months.

At the age of twenty-eight, I found myself disheartened and sad. By then I had tasted the cynicism and exploitation found in Hollywood where I lived, cracked my head soundly on the corporate glass ceiling, and had a short stint with marriage under my belt. I put myself through college selling real estate only to find at the end of my labors that horizons were limited. A bachelor's degree in English would get me a teaching job in the Watts ghetto after a two-year waiting period. I felt out of step with my peers who seemed pleased to get loaded and lay about watching dumb movies. In real estate land, people were satisfied with a check at the end of a frustrating day of sorting out other people's problems. No one seemed to share my values. It made me feel hollow. Making a living writing seemed a foolish endeavor, but wouldn't it be engaging, exciting, and rewarding! I had to know if I believed I could deliver the goods. To sort this out, I dropped out of society and landed on Kauai. Like Isabella, I fell in love with the endless beauty of the lush, life-affirming Islands.

Lured by the fiery mystery of a living volcano, Isabella took passage on the Kilauea, a well-worn steamer that ferried locals to the outer islands. She slept on the ship's skylight beneath a velvet dome pricked with stars and felt the warm trade winds. A bold-faced moon cast a path on the black water. Each breath of balmy air stirred new life within her. In Hilo, she was given a horse and told she must ride astride up the flank of the volcano to reach the summit of Mauna Loa. It was a grueling ascent through matted vines draping the ohi'a trees pricked with blood-red blossoms. Even though her body was frail, she was ecstatic to learn that while riding astride, instead of side-saddle like a well-bred lady, she was not in pain. Exhausted, yet elated at this discovery she determined to explore all the wonders of the islands on the back of a good horse.

I spent the first couple of months on Kauai on the sunny side of the island in Poipu with my head literally stuck in the sand. I absorbed the warm energy of the sun and sloshed in the azure sea. Eventually, I found lodging on the rainy north shore which was a backwater at the time. There, I shared a house with another young woman and a man who was raising his six-month-old daughter. It wasn't a commune; I paid rent and we lived individual lives. I didn't live in Kalalau where a tribe of hippies had taken up residence in a sacred Hawaiian village "living off the land" and welfare. I did visit the Taylor Camp, a notorious treehouse settlement owned by Elizabeth Taylor's brother. I took tai chi lessons, practiced yoga beneath a tin roof at a beach pavilion. I danced at Club Med which was the only nightlife in Hanalei Bay aside from the Tahiti Nui, a dim cave where bleary-eyed locals hung out. Cue the film *The Descendants* and it is now the hottest spot on the North Shore.

I met people who were cultivating spiritual journeys, eating organic vegan food, smoking red hair cannabis, getting high on magic mushrooms, surfing a lot, and playing ukuleles. My plan was to immerse myself in the beauty and raw sensuality of the island. I set a trap for lobster in the reef outside the door of my pole house at the end of tranquil Anini Road; hiked the narrow track overlooking the cobalt sea crashing upon the rugged Napali Coast up to a fern laden grotto where I swam in the alluring plunge below Hanakap'ia Falls; sat next to an expansive Hawaiian woman whose deep, powerful energy gave me the voice to sing along with her. I spent three days and three nights entirely alone in a tent on a secret beach eating fruits and nuts. This experiment was to test my own reality without the mental interference of another human. Being in this state helped me determine my true course—my own reckoning. After a blissful, meditative year in the Islands, I felt centered, replenished, and ready return to the mainland determined not to let my writing aspirations die while maintaining financial equilibrium.

After six months of harrowing and thoroughly wild horseback rides, Isabella left the healing balm of the Islands feeling invincible. She shared her exploits in her book *Six Months in the Sandwich Islands* giving me a roadmap to destinations I would I eventually explore.

I remained enchanted with the Hawaiian people and their culture, delved into their history, and made it my mission to write their story. This entailed spending nights in Waipio Valley where the sacred bones of chiefs are buried in the steep cliffs framing the valley; exploring Hilo, Puna, and Mauna Kea; having a room overlooking Kealakakua Bay where Captain Cook was killed by the natives. I tried to absorb the ancient energy at the Place of Refuge on the Big Island. I interviewed elders and read the oldest chronicles written by those alive prior to missionary contact. Isabella often stayed in rough quarters with locals, rode in a charging cavalcade up mountains, down ravines across rivers so boldly they dubbed her a *paniolo* (Hawaiian cowboy). Her unrivaled descriptions of the powerful sea, lush jungles, daunting gorges on the Hamakua Coast and mysterious Wailuku on Maui, were lifeblood for my novel *Wai-nani: A Voice from Old Hawai'i.*

While living in the Islands, I was also wrestling with the question of marriage and whether I should bring another life into the world. Isabella said if you want to be a vine winding around a tree, get married. She did not marry until she was fifty and it was to a younger man who followed her lead. I wasn't burning my bra in the streets, but I was rebelling against the traditional roles of women. It seemed the motherhood gene was missing from my DNA. It was encouraging to find a woman who had many offers of marriage but decided to follow her own destiny.

I still dream of drowsy nights listening to the waves lapping softly on the shore beneath my pole house and the trade winds lifting the palms outside my open window. The warm air perfumed by night blooming cereus and those sultry, languid days gave me solace and the strength to forge on. In 2021 I wrote and published *Embrace of the Wild,* inspired by the indomitable Ms. Bird who went on to become the best-loved travel writer of her day. She needed movement to keep her intense intellect occupied. She sailed on to San Francisco and took the train to Colorado where she rode 800 miles solo on her mountain tour. Her later years were spent in China, Japan, and Korea in places where no white woman had gone before. She was the first woman to be inducted into the Royal Scottish Geographical Society. She gave the profits from her writing to help those in need. Her gift to me was the courage to paddle my own canoe.

Meet Bennelong

We belong to the earth.
It does not belong to us
.—Aboriginal saying

Since time immemorial Tubowgule, the land on which the Sydney Opera House stands, has been a place of gathering for Aboriginal peoples. The clans would meet on the tidal island to dance, sing, feast, and share their stories. Today that piece of land that juts out into the Sydney Harbor is called Bennelong Point. On my tour of Australia, I noticed Bennelong's name popping up everywhere making me curious about what was so important about this man.

Bennelong was a notable leader of the Wangal people that lived in Manly a long canoe paddle across Sydney Harbor. I took the fast ferry ride there from Sydney Cove to spend the day exploring the popular stop. Manly Cove enjoys calm waters in the protected harbor, but a short walk across the isthmus lined with trendy shops takes you to the open sea. Surfers bob in and out of the remarkably warm rolling surf. Nearby, snorkelers ply the deep aquamarine waters where a reef provides shelter for a myriad of fishes. Much of the Manly is preserved with hiking trails leading to good viewing spots of the bay. I could see why the Aboriginal people were happy here.

In 1788 Captain Arthur Phillip landed with the First Fleet of convicts in Sydney Cove. He brought about 1,300 unfortunate men, 25 wives of these men, and about 100 prostitutes to populate the colony. This unfortunate, filthy, hungry sorry lot would be put to work building the colony. Phillip was given orders from King George III to encourage good relations with the natives. Due to an accident in Brazil, Phillips was missing a front tooth, so things started well. In the Eora tradition, a male child's transition from boyhood to manhood is marked by knocking out a front tooth. They believed this bizarre pale spirit must be a brave warrior.

Following in the wake of many of the explorers like Captain James Cook, Phillip's approach to good relations was to abduct a ruling chief to ensure civil obedience. In 1789 he sent his men to Manly where they captured Bennelong, a vital 25-year-old warrior, tied and gagged him, and took him back to the governor's home where he was to become civilized.

Bennelong had a quick mind and was curious about the ways of the whites. He allowed them to dress him in their costumes. He could be seen strolling Sydney streets wearing frilly shirts with lace cuffs and a bright red jacket with brass emulates and tight britches. He learned English and became an ambassador of the Native peoples sharing his knowledge of their culture with Phillips.

He soon became hated in both worlds. The Aboriginal people saw him as a traitor to their culture. They had witnessed the drunken, violent newcomers spreading disease among their numbers. The white convicts and indentured servants that were building the new city, eating rotting food, and wearing rags resented the black dandy strolling the streets enjoying the life of a lord. As for Bennelong, he took up residence in the governor's house, enjoyed society, and earned the reputation as a pants man.

Bennelong was allowed to visit his people in Manly and invited Captain Phillips to a feast being held there. Phillips saw this as a perfect opportunity to reconcile with Bennelong's people the fact that he had abducted their leader. As he was talking to Bennelong, a warrior inserted a ritual spear into his back. This was not a deadly strike. It was a common response to an offense committed in the Aboriginal culture to be speared! Phillips took this injury with amazing aplomb and did nothing to retaliate. Bennelong's relationship with him improved. Emboldened, Bennelong requested that Phillips build him a house on what became Bennelong's point and that his wife Barangaroo give birth to their child in the governor's house. Phillips agreed to do both conditions.

In 1792 Phillip's health failed. He returned to England taking Bennelong with him. Bennelong was put on display in the court where he held his own, especially with the ladies. He made the rounds to the usual tourist attractions and enjoyed a gracious lifestyle in England. However, in 1795 the damp climate damaged his lungs, and he became homesick.

To the shock and consternation of the English ruling the colony when Bennelong returned to Australia, he dropped his English manners. He went back to wearing a thong of kangaroo leather, painted his face, and let his full-blown hair grow. He paddled his canoe to Manly where he re-connected to the land and the ways of his people and became a respected elder in his tribe. Sadly, he developed a penchant for rum and succumbed to drunken rages. It is reported he was given to beating his wives and anyone else who got in his way. When he died in 1813, his obituary in the Sydney Gazette did not read kindly.

Of this veteran champion of the native tribe little favorable can be said. His voyage and benevolent treatment in Britain produced no change whatever in his manner and inclinations, which were naturally barbarous and ferocious.

Race relations have been slow to improve in

Australia. In 1957 landscape artist, Albert Namatjira, became the first Aboriginal man to have the right to vote and purchase a property. Before that, Aboriginal people were considered fauna with no rights. Even today, it is against the law for Aboriginal people to drink alcohol in public in some parts of the country.

Today, there have been many acts of reconciliation on the part of whites, and Aboriginals are viewed in a more charitable light. Bennelong is hailed as a bridge between the two cultures showing good humor and keen intellect. He was saddened by the horrific loss of life from smallpox and venereal disease the whites perpetrated on his people, yet he cooperated with the attempts of the English to *uplift* him.

As recently as 2018, Bennelong was given recognition for his role in the integration of the white and black people of Australia. The State Government spent 3 million dollars to purchase Putney's home that contains the gravesite of Bennelong who died at Kissing Point in Sydney.

We need to make sure we are protecting our heritage and preserving the past.—Sydney Gazette

Raven Brings the Sun

When my mother told me that at the age of 70 she was going to raft the Tatshenshini River, I didn't think much about it. She didn't mention that the head-waters of this river in the Yukon Territory of Canada flow free for 140 uninterrupted miles through a 24-million-acre roadless wilderness that encompasses the largest non-polar ice field on earth. Nor did she hint that ursus horribilis—big honkin' grizzly bears—thrive on these salmon-choked waters. Not a whisper about the apartment-building sized icebergs calving off the 20 glaciers that descend into the river that can explode into a thousand sparkling shards causing waves big enough to tip a rubber raft. She didn't chatter on about sucking holes and monster hydraulics where the Tat merges with the Alsek River to form one massive river four times the size of the Colorado. What she did say was that the Chilkat guides are real good cooks!

Now that I'd signed on to follow in her pioneering footsteps, I was not at all sure about the wisdom of this decision. The inherent dangers of bobbing for eight days in an 18-foot rubber raft on a river that goes from a 15,000 cfs joy ride to a heart-thumping 100,000 cfs flow when it meets the Gulf of Alaska, have been overridden by the desire to know the "river wild" in all its untampered grandeur. Sure, I know the mist-laden air combined with fierce winds can bring on teeth-chattering chills. But I could get lucky like Mom and see Mount Fairweather, the 15,325-foot monarch of the Saint Elias Mountains piercing indigo blue skies, flowers in riotous profusion, and a startling array of wildlife—all without mishap.

My ten fellow adventurers ranged from first-time camper to veteran river runner. Their age spread was 16 to 74. Apparently, anyone can take this trip if they can handle being without a cell phone for a week and sleeping in campsites littered with wolf, bear, and moose tracks. Our three guides expertly maneuvered our oar boats through a gauntlet of white water that would test rafters on the first day out. They avoided big holes and steered clear of bounces that would have been part of the fun in a warmer clime. The glacier silt-laden water of the Tat averages about 34 degrees; you don't want to become a swimmer. I held tightly to a strap as we blew through a chute framed by jagged buttresses. After a few smacks in the face from big waves and a bit of bailing water out of the bow of our boat, we settled into a peaceful glide.

I put my feet up on the tube, leaned back on piles of dry bags, and pulled out my binoculars to do a little birding. A chatty kingfisher took to flying along with us. Sightings of bald eagles fishing along the river became commonplace. A brownie ducked into the alders as we trundled by. Sweepers, fallen trees along the shore downed by beavers, were to be avoided.

Life on the river revolves around the movements of the curvaceous gray lady wearing a magenta sash of fireweed along her banks, locating campsites with the best views, a breeze to keep bugs at bay, and above all else the weather! The coastal Tlingit tribe of Dry Bay used the river corridor as a trade route to the interior. They believed that Raven, the creator of all things, was responsible for bringing the sun to "the people." (Tlingit means People of the Tides.) Having grown up in Haines, the prettiest little town in all southeast Alaska, I know that all of life here is driven by the weather. I purchased a "Raven Brings the Sun" T-shirt at the onset of this journey. I intended to sleep in it, eat in it, and pray in it for good measure. So far, a tender dome of blue overhead and a scintillating breeze rustling the aspen and cottonwoods that lined the shore were my reward.

A day's layover at Secret Slough, just before the confluence of the O'Connor River, meant that I would have to take a break from "having to do nothing" to enjoy Sunday morning's breakfast. Our guides set up the spotting scope so we could watch game on the braided gravel plain on the other side of the platinum Tatshenshini. Fast-moving clouds drifted about jagged peaks streaked with silver avalanche chutes for our dining pleasure. We spotted a momma moose with a calf tagging along behind. They were in a hurry, because about a 1,000-pound brownie was hot on their trail. Arctic terns fluttered over the river in search of beak-sized fish while a couple tuxedoed magpies circled our camp hoping for an easier meal.

In the early1990s, plans were afoot to shave off the top of Windy Craggy Mountain near this river confluence to get to one of the world's largest copper deposits. A bridge was to be built across Monkey Wrench rapids with a road along the Tat to the O'Connor drainage and eventual connection with the Haines Highway. Trucks carrying toxic cargo were to rumble over this road eight times a day. The tailings lake, a noxious brew of chemicals, was to be situated squarely on what is the most active seismic area in America. In 1993, Vice-President Al Gore and Canadian Premier Mike Harcourt joined forces in the fight against this folly. The silver lining of this struggle was the formation of this World Heritage Site big enough for bear, wolves, moose, wolverine, lynx, and Dall sheep to roam.

Back on the river we merged with the O'Connor and were lifted to an energetic ride through an ever-widening world. We entered a corridor of snow-laden mountains defiant in their proud beauty. Each day on the river became bigger, grander, and more overwhelmingly soothing to mind and eye.

We parked at a camp near Walker Glacier. After a ramble through a wildflower meadow spiked with crimson Indian paintbrush, yellow beach pea, and purple geranium to a ridge overlooking Walker Lake, we arrived at the snout of the glacier itself. It had receded a mile since my mother's visit 20 years ago. We crunched across the back of an ice river, hopping bottomless turquoise chasms, and stopping long enough to let a mature black bear make his way across our path.

Back in our trusty rafts, we navigated Death

Channel that opens into Alsek Lake where we bounced off berg bits on the way to our camp at Gateway Knob. The booming voices of ice spirits being freed from the calving Grand and Alsek Glaciers became our eerie music for the night. For a finale to this epic journey, Raven brought the sun shining down upon frosty Mount Fairweather. As we pulled into Dry Bay on the back of the swollen river, I had to say that Mom was right: "The Chilkat guides are real good cooks!"

On the Road with
the Lady of the Rockies

As I crested the bluff overlooking Estes Park, the summer sun pushed away the gray that had followed me from Denver (an hour's drive away) to reveal blue-bird skies. The sweet mountain town, guarded by 14,000-foot peaks of the Rocky Mountain National Park, rests in a cleft carved by the Big Thompson River. I was drawn here by the vivid descriptions of this magical place by Isabella Lucy Bird who journaled her stay as she rode 800 miles solo on her mare Birdie in 1873.

I imagined her sense of relief at having finally arrived at what she dubbed the "Inner World." She had begun her journey by train to Cheyenne, Wyoming and made her way by coach to the home of the Alexanders on the banks of the Big Thompson River in Loveland, Colorado. They were hardscrabble squatters on the land presently occupied by the Sylvan Dale Guest Ranch. Isabella was put to work washing and mending clothes and helping Mrs. Alexander with chores while she waited for a guide to take her to Estes Park. After a grueling ride and many missteps through thickly forested slopes and steep gullies, it became apparent that her guide did not know the way. Having reached an impassable box canyon framed in towering rock pinnacles, they had to turn back.

Undaunted, Ms. Bird managed to get to Longmont and an alternate route that took her up present-day Highway 36 to Estes Park. Today this bustling town is the gateway to the Rocky Mountain National Park. I enjoyed this scenic highway ramble through pine-sheathed mountains in my rental car, but nearly 150 years earlier it had taken Isabella several days to make the strenuous journey on horseback. When she arrived, the valley was spotted with the rough-hewn log cabins of settlers, hunters, and the random misanthrope.

She descended into the valley and was greeted by Mountain Jim—a desperado by her description—who charged a toll to enter nature's sanctuary. He wore animal skins crudely fashioned into clothing and a revolver at his waist. Strapped to his horse's saddle pad made from a beaver skin (complete with dangling paws) was a formidable rifle. His demeanor was calm, but his overall appearance was frightening. Blond curls to his shoulders framed a face that was strikingly handsome on one side and shockingly disfigured on the other. He had only let her see the good profile, shielding her from the fact that he only had one eye and a face badly scarred from a run-in with a bear. Although taken aback by his appearance, she let him guide her to Evans boarding house, the valley's only lodging, where she was assigned a chink-style log cabin that let the snow filter in during storms.

I felt cozy in my four-poster bed beneath a down comforter at my lodging in Estes Park, as I thought of her waking to a light blanket of snow on her covers and eyelashes crusted in frost. Strangely, this Victorian woman with delicate health found wilderness life invigorating. She felt alive and connected with the turnings of nature and enamored with the vastness of the place. Unspoiled beauty awaited her each morning and prompted her out of bed to see the sun cresting the peaks and casting a crimson glow. She had come in the autumn when burnt orange and golden willows lined the many creeks and the ground was fecund with a mat of falling leaves. She inhaled deeply the scent of pine and rose, eager to tack up Birdie and ride in the park where she met elk and deer on her hacks.

Evans owned cattle grazing land in the meadows that were once home to thunderous herds of buffalo. Since Isabella was an enthusiastic horsewoman, they offered to pay her to gather their cattle. She loved the thrill of rounding up unruly cows and was soon well-respected among the male boarders who rode with her. Lording over the pristine valley was the 14,000-

foot monarch, snow-tipped Longs Peak. As she herded cattle in the park, she became deeply immersed in the staggering beauty of the Inner World. She longed to know the vista from the stern gray face at the top of the world. She knew she couldn't go alone and asked Mountain Jim if he would take her.

I drove Trail Ridge Road in the RMNP to an overlook with a stunning view of Longs Peak and its neighbors stacked on the horizon. Though hundreds of peak baggers climb the mountain each year, I could not imagine taking up that challenge. I had hiked to pristine, glacier-fed Loch Lake resting at 10,000 feet the day before. The combination of the altitude and the stiffness of the climb had taken all my strength to get there and back. Spreading far below my vantage point were the lush green meadows where Isabella rode shod over Evans' cattle. Happily, the expansive valley is free of over-grazing today and serves to support the elk, deer, and antelope that are common sightings in the park.

Two of the early Evans' boarders had wanted to climb Longs Peak as well. Jim agreed to take them, but only if Isabella could come along. Beneath Jim's rough attire beat the heart of a gentleman. He had a civilized manner and read poetry on dark nights while sipping whiskey by the fire. He was drawn to Isabella, but knew his disfigurement was more than any woman could, or should, bear. They rode to a base camp near

Lilly Lake and made the strenuous hike from there. She was wearing her Hawaiian riding dress left over from her days riding on the Big Island (perfect for the tropics, but silly on this climb). Jim provided her with proper boots and a warm coat made from animal skins. Isabella managed to make it to the notch near the top on her own steam, but the strenuous hand-over-hand climb, combined with the altitude, made her weak and breathless. Mountain Jim did not want her to be disappointed, so he literally dragged her and, in some instances, carried her on his shoulders to the top of the world. What she saw she expressed as *"Nature, rioting in her grandest mood, exclaimed with voices of grandeur, solitude, sublimity, beauty, and infinity."*

After the arduous descent from the mountain, they sat together beside a fire gazing at shivering stars. It is a favorite rumor in the region that her gratitude to him and his admiration for her were given full reign on that night.

Isabella continued her quest to explore points south, including Denver and Boulder, Colorado. I carried on my own explorations, left the Inner World, and headed up Highway 34 toward Loveland and the Sylvan Dale Ranch where I was to spend the night. There is no mention in the guide books of the stagger-ing beauty of this drive that traces the mighty Big Thompson River. The canyon carved over the millennium by this mad rush of water through blocks of granite shooting skyward is often closed due to rock slides and flooding. This is the box canyon that had stopped Isabella short in her first attempt to reach the inner world. The road could not be engineered until 1904.

After her circuit through Colorado, Isabella returned to Evans lodge in the winter to know still beauty, silence, and solitude again. *The park below lying in intense sunlight, with all the majestic canyons which sweep down upon it in depths of infinite blue gloom, and above, the pearly peaks, dazzling in purity and glorious form, cleft the turquoise blue of the sky. How can I ever leave it?* This she asked herself in letters to her sister Henrietta back in Scotland that make up her travel memoir *A Lady's Life in the Rocky Mountains*.

Isabella Lucy Bird would be pleased to know that in spirit she never left the Inner World. Her loving descriptions helped bring attention to the spectacular region protected today from development known as the Rocky Mountain National Park. I was surprised that locals in Estes Park who had lived there many years, and the thousands of hikers who flock to the region each year to re-connect to the wild, did not know her name. Her legacy lives on with me.

Too Many Elephants in the Room

Good news: There are too many elephants!
Bad news: There are too many elephants!

With so many environmental groups fighting to prevent poaching of these impressive beasts for their ivory tusks, it is ironic that there is overpopulation in the parks I visited in Botswana, Zimbabwe, and Zambia. An estimated 130,000 elephants roam the vast, unfenced preserves under the protection of armed, patrolling rangers.

Elephants graze about 18 hours a day, each taking in about 400 pounds of grasses that the kudu, impala, sable, and other wildlife need to survive. They eat the leaves of the Mopane tree that giraffes and other creatures rely upon. Dead zones are left in their wake where they have eaten everything down to a nub and killed trees by debarking them with their tusks. This rate of unsustainable devastation will leave animals starving if something is not done to curb damage caused by the growing population of elephants clustered in southern Africa.

Michael Masukule, leader of a community adjacent to Kruger in South Africa, said, "They destroy our crops, occupy our drinking places, compete with our livestock for food, and are a danger to our people. Whatever decision you take, do not forget us people who encounter elephants every day."

Villagers live in fear of the pachyderms that plunder their crops at night leaving them without enough food for winter. Elephants have killed people living on the edge of and inside national parks when they try to stop them from eating everything in sight.

On the flight from Chobe in Botswana to Victoria Falls in Zimbabwe, we gazed upon a seemingly endless green carpet of Mopane forests pocked with the watering holes of thousands of elephants ranging here. It was hard to believe that there is not enough space to go around, but 80 percent of Botswana is desert, and the vast herds of zebra, antelope, and elephants are mainly found in the remaining 20 percent that they share with humans.

Botswana currently has the largest elephant population. In the early 1960s, there were less than 10,000 pachyderms in this landlocked and generally dry country. By 1990 there were 50,000 elephants in the wetter, northern parts of the country, and in the following year, the Botswana Department of Wildlife Conservation and National Parks drafted an elephant management policy. In that year (1991) it was established that the then-current elephant population of 55,000 was the maximum the country could sustain without the eventual loss of habitat so essential for species biodiversity.

The gigantic mammals were responsible for 67 human deaths and 26 injuries between 2009 and 2019 with the highest number of deaths caused by a wild animal in Botswana, second to the highest after leopards.

Suggested solutions to the problem included introducing birth control, but that has proven to be too expensive and impractical as the drug has to be re-injected every six months to be effective. Culling the herds is talked about in whispers, but government officials are afraid that approach will alienate visitors and might even trigger economic sanctions from other countries who are not living at the effect of the elephants, and do not understand the gravity of the situation. Culling is particularly problematic because of the legendary intelligence and memory of the elephants. If they see humans killing off family members, they are likely to become aggressive and more dangerous to villagers and tourists alike. The entire family would have to be killed, including the babies, at the same time to prevent this type of revenge. It's not feasible.

It is an uneasy co-existence. Fear of elephants has long dictated the daily behaviors of the thousands living in the villages dotting Okavanga's river banks. Villagers stay at home after sunset to avoid elephants roaming the region looking for food and water. The elephants eat the crops in their hard-earned gardens at night.

The human/elephant conflict increased in 2019 when the government of Botswana lifted a five-year ban on elephant hunting to enable farmers to protect their livelihoods and lives from elephant attacks.

My visit to the region was in 2015, and since then a system of Elephant buses has been put in place on the Okavanga river corridor. The buses pick up children in the villages and deliver them to school, so they are not walking across elephant migration trails on the way. It is a limited service that will not pick up adults unless they are medical workers. It has been a successful deterrent but is underfunded and limited in its scope. (BBC article 2022)

There are, however, some smaller steps that can be taken to minimize the effects of elephants on local crops. Elephants are afraid of bees. The installation of hives of African bees at intervals surrounding a field has effectively deterred the elephants and given the villagers income from the honey they produce. In 2002, researchers found that African elephants stay away from acacia trees with beehives. Later studies revealed that not only do the elephants run away from the sound of buzzing bees, but they also emit low-frequency alarm calls to alert family members about the possible threat. Similarly, elephants don't like chilies. Capsaicin, the chemical in chilies that make them hot, is an irritant causing elephants to cough, sneeze, and eventually turn away from crops surrounded by a buffer of chilies. (BBC article by Shreya Dasgupta 2014)

Other solutions considered are extending existing parks through more land acquisitions, moving more elephants from overpopulated to underpopulated parks, and opening corridors between parks to allow elephants to resume some of their old migration routes. Enter KAZA TFCA—the Trans Frontier program that opens up migration routes crossing international borders. This initiative of the governments of Angola, Botswana, Namibia, Zambia, and Zimbabwe was formulated in 2012. It involves the land situated in the Okavango and Zambezi river basins where the borders of the five countries converge. The five countries have come together to solve the problems of shrinking habitats and hideous poaching that crosses international borders. Implementing the good intentions of this agreement has proven to be difficult. The elephants are not cooperating. They are remaining clustered in parks like Hwange in Zimbabwe where there are man-made watering holes to sustain them throughout the dry season.

"KAZA is a wonderful idea whose success will be determined in decades rather than years. This region is very dry and has limited water resources.

The elephant is a water-dependent species. Getting elephants to move (migrate) may very well be impossible as they follow the memories of the matriarch(s) who may have not learned a migratory pattern. Just because KAZA is implemented doesn't mean the elephants can take advantage of it. They are at the mercy of the elements and their needs. Shutting down the man-made resources might stimulate elephant movement, but it will also cause tourism to suffer, one of the main reasons for the treaty being created." (Mat Dry, Safari Guide, author of *This is Africa*, and owner of TIA Safaris)

Meanwhile, Mother Nature has come up with a plan of her own for herd reduction. Four hundred elephant deaths were recorded in 2022. This is attributed to cyanobacteria, a microscopic organism related to climate change. Not all cyanobacteria produce toxins, but scientists say toxic ones are occurring more frequently as climate change drives up global temperatures.

This article is not designed to diminish or minimize the efforts of conservationists fighting to prevent the slaughter of elephants for their ivory tusks in parks ravaged by poachers. That horrendous disregard for life must stop. However, Africa is an enormous continent and what is true in the Congo and other parts of Africa is not the reality in other countries. Outsiders should understand that if culling becomes the only answer to this problem, it will not happen before all else fails. But, again, this situation is not sustainable for the other animals in the parks or for the humans living in and/or on the edge of the last great wild places in Africa.

Was it Worth It?

This is the question I asked a woman standing in line with me and about another hundred people to board the shuttle to trailheads in the Rocky Mountain National Park outside of Estes Park. I was doubtful that I could enjoy hiking trails with the herds; not that I am anti-social, but I go to the woods to pull the plug on society and reconnect with nature. Big and small were lined up with backpacks, walking sticks, strollers, and children in tow. I was also concerned about the elevation gain in the hikes in the Colorado Rockies. Since I am a Lost Angel from sea level, I am susceptible to altitude sickness and get a throbbing headache and nausea around 9,000 feet.

"No worries," she said. "The crowds thin out as you get higher in the mountains. Why don't you get off at the Glacier Gorge stop and hike up to Loch Lake? By the time you get to the top, you might have it all to yourself."

I popped off the shuttle at Glacier Gorge hoping for the best. The first leg of the inviting path took me over a footbridge crossing a chuckling creek lined with lush grasses and fern fronds. The well-maintained track followed a gorge livened by the deep voice of an energetic river. A brilliant sun in a blue canopy was tempered by cotton candy clouds drifting overhead while a flirtatious breeze lulled me into forgetting how intense the sun can be. Soon I was cooling my jets beside Alberta Falls, a powerful surge of the water charging down a granite flume and sending a cooling spray. This stop bolstered me for the next two miles of a steady upward climb.

The striated, glistening mineral walls of the gorge

drew early settlers in search of gold. I was here because I wanted to know firsthand what inspired Isabella Lucy Bird to ride solo in the Rockies in 1873. She was a plucky English woman who came to Colorado for the "cure." Many people with asthmatic conditions came here to escape the sooty, damp air of London and to breathe deeply of the thin, dry air of Colorado. She was not, however, content to stay in a sanitarium in Denver; she needed to explore. In letters to her sister in Scotland, she described the harsh conditions she endured to know the ephemeral beauty of the high country. I am toying with the idea of writing a historical novel based on her life and wanted to get inside her mindset.

It seems I have the same *need to see the world* gene in my DNA. I am fully engaged in the state of exploration; however, shortly I found myself sitting down in the shade to catch my breath and let my beating heart calm down. I started to recognize other hikers I had passed on the way as they overtook me and kept climbing steadily upward. I had taken Diamox, a prescription drug that minimizes the symptoms of altitude sickness. Though feeling a bit shaky and inadequate, I was determined to reach the lake. The trail was lined with all manner of wildflowers: rock rose, spring vetch, and my favorite powder-blue columbine. Aspens with spinning chartreuse leaves and Ponderosa pine provided shade. I would not let my frailty prevent me from seizing this stunning day.

This went on for an hour or two. I would keep climbing on the rocky stepped trail until I needed to sit for about ten minutes. I kept drinking water knowing that it is easy to become dehydrated in the dry air of Colorado. The noonday sun now burned brightly, and the shady trees had disappeared. I was on a narrow trail hugging a ledge overlooking the river a thousand feet below. My fingertips were tingling; I was becoming alarmed.

"Was it worth it?" I asked a young woman on her way back down the path from the lake.

"You are only three switches away, about a half mile. Don't give up," she said brightly.

Giving up is not in my nature, but my fingertips were vibrating with pulsing blood. This gave me pause. The Diamox was having a violent reaction. It can also make a person more sensitive to the sun. Maybe the doctor had given me too strong a dose. I could only hope it was that and not heat stroke setting in. Any reasonable person would have turned around.

But I couldn't.

"Was it worth it?" I asked another hiker coming down the steep switchbacks.

"My wife came from Germany to hike this trail," he said in a thick accent. She was marching behind him placing her walking stick with firm conviction.

"Yes, it was worth it!" she beamed.

With this encouragement, I pressed on and kept

asking the same question of hikers as they descended the narrow track. I was inwardly hoping someone would tell me it wasn't, and then I could turn back down the mountain. I was exhausted. My knees and ankles were caving in. I was perspiring heavily, and I felt light-headed. Snow patches appeared on the trail and trickles of melting snow made for a slippery climb.

"How high are we?" I ventured. "I die at about 9,000 feet."

"About 10,000," said a young woman who seemed unfazed.

The trail finally crested to overlook a staggeringly beautiful glacier-fed lake framed in stern granite peaks mottled with snow. My water was depleted, and I felt near starving. A family of four having their picnic on the shore offered to filter the water for me. We shared our delight at being here on this glorious day. Soon our boots were off, and we were dangling our feet in shockingly cold water. We exchanged goodies in our lunch bags and laughed about the challenges of the climb. My lunch companions got creative with cell phone snaps providing further proof that I had made it to Loch Lake.

Isabella's rapturous, unrestrained delight in this region that gave her "cheerful good health" brought me here. The majesty of Loch Lake did not disappoint. Mountain trout swam in the placid, chill waters. Breathing deeply of the crystalline air left me amazingly refreshed.

It may have not been smart to press on considering the tingling in my hands and that it took five hours to do a three or four-hour hike, but, my friends, IT WAS WORTH IT! It gave me a deep sense of accomplishment and proved to me that I can handle altitude if I am careful and go slowly. I recounted the many warm hellos and helping hands along the way. The herds of people I once dreaded on that overstuffed shuttle who made this climb had become allies in my quest to know what made Isabella and millions more seek the blissful state found in the high country.

The Enemy

My yearning for genuine, unhurried solitude brought me to a strip of sand beneath a canopy of wind-blown trees bereft of leaves at Emma Woods Beach Park in Ventura, California. As I lay belly down listening to the rhythm of the rolling waves and letting the wind lick my legs, I spied a homeless man curled in the armpit of a protective dune. I hoped that he could actually sleep there nestled in the ice plant and that some authority would not challenge his grimy gray existence and tell him to move along. He lifted his stocking-capped head from his knapsack and looked at me from below a band of bright orange.

Not wanting to encourage an incident with more than split-second eye contact, I consciously collected my yoga mat and headed for a more populated section of the beach. So much for solitude, but today is today. As I strode past the man, I chanced a glance over my shoulder. Indeed he was sitting up now, watching me. How do I answer this gaze? Shall I avoid insulting him by calmly conveying I had a change of mind about this spot, or shall I display a modicum more of assertiveness to squelch any ideas of advance he may be having?

I plodded into the wind until I reached a vacant patch close to a couple enraptured with each other's harmonica playing abilities. Better than families with too many young children; better than smokers or chatting girls. The moody morning slipped into a sparkling afternoon while I lazed away the day.

Sad to leave sand and surf behind, I stood, stretched, and headed in the direction of my car. When in I reached in my pocket for the keys I found, to my horror, they were not there. I backtracked in my mind every step I had taken that day. As I hurried along, I recalled making a quick stop at the restroom before going to the beach. If I left my keys on the sink, they could have been discovered. Similarly, my stash-filled wallet, lightly concealed in the trunk, would be easy pickings for the devious. I felt a clutching at the base of my throat. Breathless at the thought of having no car, no cell phone, and no money, I wondered what a night on the dunes would be like.

Hurrying through a dark tunnel beneath train tracks to the restroom, I was much relieved to see my car still parked in the deserted lot. I slowed to a walk to catch my breath. When I reached the restroom, I flung its door open. My heart sank to my flip-flops upon seeing that my keys were not there. I moved toward my car hoping I had simply left the keys in the ignition, but I could see from twenty yards out that all buttons were down; the doors were locked. Now what?

As I contemplated my alternatives, I heard someone call "yoo-hoo." Fairly nearby, a grizzled man sitting on the picnic table waved something with a bright flash of orange in one hand and tinkled my set of keys like a bell in the other.

"Looking for these?"

My heart first froze, and then began to sing like Julie Andrews in a movie. I bounced over to the man in what felt like cinematic slow motion. His jeans were indeed grayed by grime, but he rose to his feet in a gentlemanly way, and smiled with orange/brown tobacco stained teeth. I realized that he was the vagrant I had seen in the dunes. Behind his red-rimmed eyes there sparkled a gentle, sad light. I grabbed his crusty hand and pumped it with all my strength.

"Thank you. Thank you so much," I said.

"I saw you on the beach. Figured you'd have to come back sometime," he said.

"You could have stolen my car, taken everything I have."

"I'm no thief ma' am," is all he said.

"No. No you're not. Please… please let me give you something," I said.

He followed me back to my car. I opened the trunk to find my wallet and handed him a twenty.

"Is this enough?" I asked.

"Lord, thank you Jesus, I sure do need this!"

We shook again, my lotion-soft hand in his weathered mitt, both of us filled with genuine gratitude for the other's existence. I got into my car, sped through the parking lot, and waved a hearty goodbye. He returned the gesture with equal vigor.

Tears of relief welled and rolled down my cheeks all the way to Ojai where I had homemade ice cream and wondered should I have given more.

Part Two

DESTINATIONS TO DIE FOR

Eyes on Africa's Wild Places

With eyes peeled for game, we did the African mambo through deeply rutted sand tracks of the Okavango Delta in Botswana while morning mists rose over the golden savannah. Our guides, Cowboy and Wise Guy, stopped the land rovers filled with 15 guests eager for adventure to read the morning headlines. Tracks in the powdery sand told them lion had passed this way in the night.

"Hold on," called Cowboy as he lurched off road and charged through thickets, knocking over young mopane trees and fording deep gullies carved by hippo. After 45 minutes of heart-thumping pursuit, our guides circled our wagons around a pride of five magnificent lions sprawled in tall grasses resting after a night of hunting. A majestic male with a dark brown mane and orange eyes stared at us with utter disdain. His mate and their two adolescent daughters remained in quiet repose as we snapped our cameras like paparazzi.

Our bush camp, located in the largest inland delta in the world, is part of a private reserve leased from the Kwai villagers. Unlike in the national parks in Africa, we were allowed to off-road and track game and take photos. (Shooting game is outlawed anywhere in Botswana.) We crossed the bridge on the River Kwai to cruise the floodplain where crocs lay in wait for the careless red lechwe, impala, or puku grazing on the shore. A couple secretary birds and the giant hornbill and saddleback cranes poked the grasses for frogs as a water monitor lizard slithered by.

We stopped for lunch at a waterhole where a band of big boys was swilling water with massive trunks. Young male elephants are cast out of the herd and stay together for many years learning what it takes to be a dominant male. A learned matriarch oversees females and the young. There were many baby elephants in the parades that we saw that day. At our sundowner, the ritual happy hour of the bush selected for the best spot to view the orange sun dropping on the black horizon, we witnessed elephants charging across a meadow, trumpeting and flapping their ears wildly as they chased a hyena away from a two-month-old baby.

Each of the four bush camps visited on the Ultimate Safari (a 17-day, all-inclusive holiday offered by Overseas Adventure Travel) is set in unique microclimates. They are similar in that the main lodge with a thatched roof, teak wood floors, and open beams serves as a meeting place and dining hall where delicious buffet meals are served. Screened-in tent homes with all the amenities including private baths and electricity provide glamping at its best. Guests are greeted with dancing and drumming and the three-night stay ends with a traditional ceremony around the fire in the boma. Hosts are gracious, extending, and eager to please. The influence of the British colonists is seen in formal table settings and high tea at 3:00 p.m. each day.

Our first camp on the edge of Chobe National Park in Botswana, the third largest preserve in Africa, overlooked the Chobe River where the flamingo-pink sunset framed in gold stained the water magenta. Sightings included numerous elephants, herds of impala (the fast food of the savannah), handsome kudu with his elegant curling antlers, the bad-tempered Cape buffalo, wart hogs running with tails held high, and a journey of gangly giraffes frolicking around the Chobe River that was lined with avocet, Egyptian geese, herons, and egrets.

In Zambia, we enjoyed a dreamy day beneath tender blue skies on the Kafue River where it merges with the Lafupa. Birders like me were excited to be on the slow boat—a pleasant change from the rocking and rolling in safari vehicles on dirt roads during game drives. Fisher people shot up the river on a fast boat and came home with buckets of tilapia and catfish. Hippos blew bubbles and yawned through gaping mouths as we floated past their watery home. Jacana walking on the lily pads with huge white blooms and flashy malachite kingfishers kept us company on our glide past Waterbury trees and unlikely palms lining the shore. While resting that afternoon in my screened-in tent home on the bank of the Lafupa, a troop of vervet monkeys peered in at me with quizzical faces. Wildlife in the camps is commonplace. I went to sleep one night listening to the belly rumblings of elephants, another the pounding hooves of a herd of buffalo, and at the river camp the grunts of the hippos that sounded like they were laughing at us.

At Hwange in Zimbabwe, our lodge sat on the edge of an escarpment overlooking basalt mopane woodland stretching to the horizon. Our game drive here garnered a cheetah strolling casually across a dead zone created by the many elephants that munch the leaves of the mopane trees and tear at the bark of the upside-down baobab trees with their tusks. At our lunch stop at the Masuma Pan watering hole, a mena-gerie of animals that would fill Noah's Ark grazed casually at the water's edge. A parade of elephants sauntered in for a drink while chuffing impala let us know that big cats were nearby. Zebras, kudus, hippos, crocs, giraffes, and baboons all came to the party.

Victoria Falls—a wild, untamable torrent that charges through a deep gorge sending spray 1,500 feet into the air—was a grand finale to our tour. Mist from the falls nourishes a rainforest of tropical foliage that seems out of place in what is mostly an arid region. A path tracing the gorge takes you to Dangerous Point where a deluge drenches the undaunted tourist. I lunched on crocodile salad on the terrace of the Victoria Falls Hotel overlooking the falls where heads of nations come to relax in a remnant of the colonial splendor. You can see the smoke and hear the thunder of the falls in the distance while giving homage to a body of water that knows no master. Activities offered at Victoria Falls are helicopter rides, white water rafting on the lower Zambezi River (not for the faint-hearted), and elephant-back safaris. On our last night, we enjoyed a dinner cruise on the upper Zambezi with a copper sunset farewell.

Sacha Lodge, Ecuador –
It's a Jungle Out There

The Earth has music, for those who listen.
—William Shakespeare

I leaned back on the comfy seat of my canoe shared with five other travelers in the magical maze of canals at Sacha Lodge in the Ecuadorian Amazon basin and watched a troop of squirrel monkeys overhead. With death-defying leaps, they sprang from branch to branch forming a superhighway through the tropical foliage. Bets were taken on who would become the first to have a monkey land on their head as the creatures peered at us with the comical faces of a curious child. After four days of total immersion in the rainforests surrounding the lodge, I felt I was a part of this scene.

This adventure begins in Coca, a gritty oil town, where the Coca and Napo Rivers collide and proceed to the mighty Amazon. A motorized canoe awaited us on the banks of the Napo, the main artery in the region. On the way to the lodge about three hours downstream, we passed barges carrying heavy equipment to oil depots and locals in canoes fishing as they have done for thousands of years. Children waved to us as we passed remote villages tucked in the impenetrable sea of green foliage. We hiked on a boardwalk through a flooded forest to Pilchicocha Lake, aka the Black Lagoon, where canoes and guides were waiting. After a serene glide over the lake lined with rhododendron leaves as big as elephant ears and reeds where Caiman (a member of the alligator family) lurk, we arrived at the miracle of Sacha Lodge.

Nestled in a 5,000-acre preserve, this Robinson

Crusoe fantasy made from local wood, covered in a shaggy palm roof, and staffed by 65 indigenous workers, is totally self-sufficient. The lounge upstairs overlooking the lagoon is cooled by most-welcome fans after a session of hiking in equatorial heat. Raised walkways lead to spacious rooms with open beam, wood floors, and inviting hammocks on the deck. There is nothing but a screen between you and the wild mishmash of jungle trees and plants that are home to millions of thrumming insects, barking tree frogs, clicking cicadas, and the sharp whistles of birds whose chorus intensifies as night draws nigh.

An early rise increases chances of spotting wildlife and some of the 600 species of birds counted at the lodge. Forest walks are the classroom for naturalist guides who point out the medicinal properties in plants and how they were used by "the people." Our guide explains the symbiotic relation-ships between plants and insects that have evolved over the ages. He carries an iPod with calls to attract the mot mots, toucans, and a variety of birds while talking to other creatures in their language trying to draw them near.

"Friends, look at this mandible ant," our guide Marco said as he pointed to a stream of insects on the jungle floor. "He can be used to suture wounds. Just let him clamp the wound with his mandible and then pinch off his head."

"Friends, you see the Kapok tree? This one is centuries old. He is the tallest tree of the jungle. If he were to be cut down, it would take a hundred years for the forest floor to recover. His canopy provides shade for the plants below. Competition for light and nutrients is fierce in the rain forest."

Like Jack on the beanstalk, we climbed a giant wooden stairwell wrapping the Kapok tree. A drenching rain set in before we reached a viewing platform above the protective canopy. We stood atop what must be listed as the 9th wonder of the world with our heads tucked into the hood of our ponchos waiting for the weather to change. Soon enough, blue skies opened over the platinum Napo River. Pink flamingo hues softened gray layers of clouds. Shafts of light streamed down upon the primal forest and mist began to rise from the verdant canopy of the forest below. Orange, crimson, and yellow blooms that rest on the crown of trees brightened the scene. Birds begin to stir once again. A flock of toucans flew swiftly by, and the song of the industrious weaverbird was heard. The sun set with a tender sigh in soft pastels as we left our perch and canoed home through the tranquil channels to the lodge and another fabulous meal.

Healthful salads of shredded cabbages, carrot, tree tomatoes, and avocado served with a tangy lime dressing were just a few of the choices. Entrees include tender beef in a peppercorn sauce, chicken, pork, and tilapia prepared with unique seasonings known only to our native chef. The meal was topped off with wonderful desserts like strawberry mousse, flan, exotic fruits, and walnut cakes served buffet style in the lodge.

On our night canoe, the heavens opened wide with a neon crescent moon hanging in a crackling sky. Marco pointed out different constellations with his powerful green laser. Glittering eyes of the caymen alligators hidden in the reeds near the shore watched our night ride. The glide around the lake in splendid silence looking up to the southern sky listening to the serenade of the cicadas and frogs is a treasured memory.

Thankfully, there are no radios or televisions, no boom boxes, no leaf blowers, or car alarms at Sacha. The promise is that the lodge will build more exciting features like the longest (1,000 ft.) and highest (120 ft.) canopy walk unique to Ecuador, the Kapok Tower, and trails that enable people to experience the forests in an intimate way, but they will not add to the 26 private rooms ensconced in green. This spectacular eco-lodge exists because of the dream of Arnold Ammeter, more commonly known as Benny. It will remain if it is protected from encroachment of oil companies that cut roads into the forest creating access for poachers and inevitable spills that threaten the entire Amazon basin.

Tango to Trekking
in the Lake District of Argentina

Church bells ring outside my window and remind me that Buenos Aires is a strongly Catholic town. Pope Francis is from Buenos Aires and he returns here to speak at the Metropolitan Cathedral, considered the heart of the city—a city that is a frenetic beehive of activity. One must cross the busy boulevards with extreme caution because the constant flow of huge trucks, tourist busses, commuters in economy cars, and thousands of scooters bolting in and out will not stop. It is up to you to navigate streaming hordes of pedestrians on their way to who-knows-where in a hurry. July 9, the busy six-lane motorway with a tree-studded median and greenbelts, is so named because that date marks the day that Buenos Aires got its independence from Spain.

The four million people who live in the city proper are mostly Spanish with an Italian accent. The result is a devilishly handsome, passionate, animated population. In the turn of the century there was a program put forth by the government to encourage workers to come from Europe promising them land and a future. Six million took advantage of this generous offer that turned out to be a false promise. Many stayed and made their way, but just as many returned to their homelands. The result is a cosmopolitan city with European architecture, a host of art galleries, and a thriving theater district. Porteños, as the people of Buenos Aires prefer to call themselves, are very proud of Teatro Colón (the Colon opera house) touted as possessing the best acoustics of any opera house in the world.

A stroll along the Rio Plata (river of silver) on a balmy summer eve brings to mind a night in Paris. The lights strung on the yachts tied along the dock and atop the Women's Bridge reflect the many colors of the city in the river below. Young and old lovers stroll hand and hand while tango dancers and musicians add to the romance in the air.

Bariloche, a two-hour flight away in the Lake District of Argentina, is where Porteños go for a respite from the city. In the early 1900s, Perito Moreno, a geographer and naturalist, rode here with our very own Teddy Roosevelt. Under his influence, Lake Nahuel Haupi (pronounced Noel Wapi), the heart of the Lake District, and 3,000 scenic square miles of surrounding forest were designated Argentina's first national park. The rich and varied landscape of lakes, glacier-fed rivers, and meadows is laced with hiking trails and campgrounds. My gracious, old world hotel sat high on a knoll overlooking manicured grounds framed in blood red roses and this gorgeous region with hiking, boating, fishing, horseback riding, river rafting, and skiing options.

Founded in 1902, San Carlos de Bariloche was first populated by colonies of Swiss, Italian, and Germans. In an attempt to re-create the alpine resorts at home, they planted evergreen trees like Douglas fir, cypress, and flowering plants that love abundant rainfall. Today, mounds of cheery yellow Scotch Broom brighten the shoulder of the two-lane highway wrapping the immense lake. Meadows are infested with lupine. Swiss chalets are at home here and dark chocolate is the town's claim to fame.

A chairlift to a ski hut provided a panoramic view of the Moreno and Nahuel Haupi lakes framed in mountains sheathed in green. We took a walk in an indigenous forest with our naturalist guide. There were few blooming plants with the Amazon fig-like tree predominant. This was followed by an energetic hike through a bouquet of introduced wildflowers to a vista of the fingers of the lake framed in snow-streaked peaks.

The early settlers had a pension for beer. We visited a microbrewery where a young man explained to us the detailed process of making his artisan beer.

He uses water fresh from the nearby glaciers that form in the towering rock faces surrounding his valley. He goes to a valley surrounded by mountains protected from the fierce winds and stinging rains to get his hops. His father owns the adjoining rustic restaurant with rough-hewn beam ceilings and hundreds of empty bottles framing the bar. The sun glistened on the leaves shiny from a recent rain while we enjoyed a warming lamb stew with a delicious squash soup for a starter and chocolate ice cream with a raspberry topping for dessert.

On the north shore of Nahuel Kwe took a lonely drive on a dirt road tracing a rushing creek to an estancia where we were treated to a traditional asado (barbeque) of beef, lamb, and sausages. Stunted shrubs spiked with flaming firebush brought Wyoming to mind. Plots of land 10,000 acres strong were given to early settlers. It's rumored that Butch Cassidy, Etta Place, and the Sundance kid hung out here at one of the estancias in between bank robberies. I can understand why they felt at home in these wide-open spaces.

Falldorado in the Front Range with Isabella Bird

I set out to trace Isabella's hoofprints through the Front Range where she rode 800 miles solo though the high country in the winter of 1873. The day broke clear when I headed up Highway 285 which was the Denver Stage Road in Isabella's day. It is a sweeping highway that curls through forests of ponderosa pine with splotches of orange willows and lemon-colored aspen on the left and the energetic Platte River on the right. The drive crests with a view of South Park, a vast and desolate plain blasted by howling winds.

In need of company in this lonely expanse, Isabella followed a stranger who turned out to be Comanche Bill, a notorious Indian killer. She shared the trail with him through Terryall Valley where gold was discovered in 1859. I followed their tracks though this rust-colored valley watered by a stealthy stream. Weathered cabins likely built in her day spoke of the hard times of miners who rushed the valley in search of treasure. Bill directed her to Fairplay, my next stop.

Isabella rode an average of 25 miles a day stopping when she saw a light through a cabin's window. Knocking on the doors of strangers to get out of the weather and being invited in and fed, she often slept with the children. I settled into my cozy room at the Hand Hotel built in 1879 wondering how she could have managed that rough life. Isabella spoke of ruffians and vigilante law in this stop in time. Today there is an outdoor western museum where one can wander among 43 structures built in the 1800s relocated here at great expense. For ten bucks you may survey this expansive exhibit for as long as you like.

On the way to trendy Breckenridge, I saw swaths of aspen carving a path through the deep green of the pine-sheathed peaks. This stretch on Highway 9 is a bit of a nail-biter with dizzying descents and tricky hairpin turns, but worth the butterflies. I stopped for a leg stretch on the charming river walk in Brecken-ridge. When rain drops started falling on my head, I pressed on toward Highway 119, the glorious Peak to Peak Highway.

A stop at Georgetown, home to the most restored Victorian homes in the state, garnered a barbeque lunch to fortify me for the rest of the drive. The popular Georgetown narrow gauge rail that puffs its way through the aspen and pines is an adventure anyone can enjoy. Isabella came through here on her way to

Green Lake. She was warned off making the climb but was undaunted. When she arrived at her ultimate destination after an arduous slog through snowdrifts, the lake was frozen solid.

A short hop from Georgetown through Central City to the Peak to Peak Highway delivers you to Estes Park where Isabella began and ended her mountain tour. It is a spectacular cruise through some of Colorado's most glorious scenery. Averaging 25 miles a day on her steadfast mount Birdie, Isabella accomplished her mountain tour in about a month. On especially horrible days she would ride fifty miles to reach a cabin with a light on where she could stay the night. After seeing the vast expanses through some of our country's most daunting land-scapes, my admiration for this indomitable woman has only deepened.

I agree with Isabella: The Front Range with its dramatic descents, charging rivers, and austere granite peaks is not to be missed, but Estes Park remains the fairest. It is the gateway to the Rocky Mountain National Park with miles of well-groomed trails to lakes and waterfalls for all to enjoy. I was well-received at the YMCA Library where I shared a power point presentation about my mountain tour. Steaming away in the lodge's spa, I felt gratified to know I was welcome here. As the aspen trees swayed and shimmied in a brisk wind, I drifted away dreaming of my return to Colorado.

Isabella Bird is considered to be the Mother of the RMP because her powerful descriptions brought throngs of tourists and writers like me to know what she described so lovingly in letters to her sister Henrietta in 1873. Her book *A Lady's Life in the Rockies* is still in print today.

The Devil Made Me Do It!

Eager to hike the trails in Eagle Hawk Nest on the Tasman Peninsula, I set out early from Hobart, the largest port and gateway to adventures in Tasmania. The intoxicating perfume of wildflowers drifting on a sea breeze greeted when I pulled over to view the shimmering blue Tasman Sea far below. The Waterfall Bay Walk was a perfect amble through the forest overlooking the craggy rock formations and aquamarine coves far below. Three Capes Track, a four-day, 30-mile track skirting the soaring dolerite cliffs unveiled in 2015, draws trekkers from around the globe. I left regretting I had not allotted more time to explore this gorgeous region. I gave myself one week in Tasmania (fast becoming a mecca for outdoor enthusiasts) to hit the top sites of Cradle Mountain National Park, Cataract Gorge in Launceston, and Wineglass Bay in Freycinet National Park on the sunny east coast, so it was time to go.

A three-hour drive north of Hobart through the arid middle of the country brought me to my friends' home in Launceston. Proud of the rich heritage of their city, they pointed out the many Victorian structures and remnants of the convict days and gardens that grace their city. They took me to a gracious restaurant overlooking the Cataract Gorge, famous for hikes into the dramatic canyon carved by the Esk River that is traversed by a striking suspension bridge.

From there I drove the winding road to Cradle Mountain, stopping in Deloraine for a "toastie" (a grilled/panini-like sandwich) and tea. A river walk in drizzling rain reminded me of the Mother Country. Its tidy patchwork quilt of pastures on rolling hills dotted with sheep completed the picture; the difference being this bucolic scene is framed in ragged spires.

The country lane soon turned into a corkscrew affair that spiraled upward through mountains sheathed in thick forests. No one had mentioned to me that Tasmania is one of the most mountainous islands in the world. Accidents on the narrow lanes are common. You are advised not to drive after dusk as that is when the wombats, wallabies, and pademelons come out to graze causing accidents as people swerve to miss them. The nocturnal Tasmanian Devil, rarely seen outside of sanctuaries, is coming back from the brink of extinction. The devils suffer from an infectious viral cancer in the form of a facial tumor that spreads through biting and has killed 90 percent of them in the wild.

Cradle Mountain National Park is home to the highest peaks in Tasmania with wild, unpredictable weather. Even though it was raining the day I arrived, I attempted to hike the 4-mile Dove Lake Circuit. The trailhead is also where the challenging 6-day Overland Track begins. Sheets of water shut out the view of the mountains framing the lake and forced me to turn back. I was, however, able to enjoy the Enchanted Woods track in the gloom of a haunting forest ensconced in moss and algae to energetic Knyvet Falls.

Another roller coaster road brought me to the sunny east coast of Tasmania where endless miles of white sand beaches are kissed by turquoise rollers off the Tasman Sea. Sailboats dot the marinas and summer cottages line the shore of coastal villages. My charming Airbnb in Bicheno was a skip away from a blow hole, and a walk on granite rocks covered with orange lichen that brought me to a tiny marina where the special was a zesty seafood bouillabaisse. The guide on a glass bottom boat tour of the marina informed us that the marine creatures here, like squid and seahorses, are endangered due to a warm current coming from mainland Australia that is heating up the waters killing the kelp forests. Yet another imbalance in nature caused by global warming.

Freycinet National Park, home to the spectacular Wine Glass Bay, is the most popular attraction on the east coast. I took the spiraling road up to the Tourville Lighthouse where an easy loop affords mind-expanding views of the blue veil of the Tasman Sea. The marine preserve below the surface, established in 2007, begins three miles offshore and extends for 200 nautical miles to protect migrating whales and all manner of sea life in the submerged mountain range. The easiest way to experience Wine Glass Bay is to take the water taxi out of Cole's Bay. It takes you around the peninsula, drops you off on a flat trail across the isthmus to Hazards Beach where you are picked up for the return ride.

With 40 percent of the land in this island state preserved with 880 tracks lacing the national parks, Tasmania is one of the last holdouts for true conservation. The caring population of just over half a million are doing all they can to keep their home clean and green. I'm grateful to the devil that got into me and told me I had to see Tassie for myself.

Riding Off the Grid in British Columbia

I awoke to a loon's haunting call floating over the still waters of Chilko Lagoon mirroring granite spires sporting snow in July. The smell of crackling bacon and camp coffee pulled me out of my snug sleeping bag.

On the far shore, a moose with her gangly calf trotting behind was the morning news. We were totally unplugged at base camp for the pack trip out of Tyslos Park Lodge through the rugged wilderness of the Chilcotin/Cariboo region.

In the crisp morning air with dew lifting from grassy meadows, seven riders, four pack horses, and two guides headed out for Goat Camp. This is not just a ride, it is a journey back into a time when you could ride for days and see no one. Like Indians on horseback, we rode in silence through a grove of quaking aspen to a rocky shore of the Chilko Lake to water the horses. The trail to Goat Camp is infrequently used each season and feels a bit like bush-whacking. It snakes through alder thickets and then begins to climb. Our sturdy, sure-footed horses took on the steep ascent with aplomb.

Josh, our accomplished guide, encouraged us. "Stand up. Get out of the saddle. Grab mane if you have to! You don't want to sore up your horses on the climbs." He was gentle with the animals and displayed a kind spirit and a helping hand to guests. With our safety in mind, he checked cinches and made sure all was secure before leading us along narrow tracks overlooking a charging river, splashing through creeks, and clamoring up and down steep ravines.

After breaking for lunch in a lush meadow peppered with purple lupine, we continued on to reach

Goat Camp at 6,800 feet elevation. We had climbed 3,000 feet and now the air was crisp with temps hovering around 70 degrees. This magical setting was to be our home for the next three nights. I awoke here to the energetic voice of Pink Creek (so named as the minerals from the glacier feeding the stream turn it a salmon color). A favorite day ride was up the emerald green valley and across Pink Creek to its headwaters. Chartreuse alpine sedges and mosses lined the shore where it merged with a translucent glacier flow.

The day rides without the pack horses to the top of the world are nothing short of spectacular! We charged through boughs of jack pine keeping a sharp eye out for trees that can catch and bruise a knee. The forest floor was a carpet of salmonberry, devil's club, huckleberry, cinquefoil, paintbrush, columbine, rock rose, and lavender asters along with many varieties of ferns and mosses. We hopped a sparkling rill stealing through an alpine meadow and began the switch-backing trail through loose scree. Once aloft at about 8,000 feet, the air became rarified. The head-spinning 360-degree view of snow-frosted peaks and the azure Chilko Lake below was worth the climb.

On the descent back to the lagoon, I dreamed of the cooling dip awaiting me. That night we were graced with a bold blood moon with a rosy halo. I felt privileged to be here in one of the great wilderness areas of North America and to have experienced it in such a special way. After contentious conservation battles that lasted years, the rights to this region were given to the First Nation people in 2004. I hope that they will continue to choose to preserve this land that is held sacred to them.

Pack trips to the Potato and Goat camps only go out a couple times a season. They call for a modicum of fitness, a willingness to help others, the ability to tack your horse, and a desire to see this gorgeous region up close and personal. The undulating 25-mile ride back to the lodge through forests of fir and sun-drenched wildflower meadows is a fitting finale to the week on horseback.

If you prefer shorter rides with lodge comforts that include gourmet meals and a spa on the deck overlooking the pastoral valley and Chilko Lake, "lodge riding" might be a perfect fit for you. Riders from around the world seeking the most authentic riding experience gather here forming a stimulating international crowd. Many do the two-week combination with one week-long pack trip and one week of lodge riding. Non-riders come to Tyslos for fly fishing. A 21-mile float down the Chilko River garners rainbow trout, bull trout, and salmon in the fall. Photographers from around the globe gather here to capture images of the over 100 grizzly bears that call Chilko Valley home during the fall sockeye salmon run. Autumn is a lovely time of year to be here when the aspen is spinning gold.

Whatever your reason for coming, you will never forget your stay at Tyslos Park Lodge. That it exists in this remote region is a testimony to the resilience and fortitude of the McLean family. Many others have tried and failed to tame the Chilcotin Plateau— a land of extremes and endless beauty.

Footloose on the Central Coast

When rubbing shoulders with eleven million people gets too close, I turn off my cell phone, put my birding glasses in my fanny pack, and head up Highway 101. This trip, I decided to explore trails near Morro Bay, one of the top ten birding sites in the United States. This sweet fishing town, situated nicely between spectacular hiking opportunities, makes a good home base. To the south, Montana de Oro, the mountain of gold, at 8,000 acres, is one of the largest parks in the state and one of its best-kept secrets. Fifty miles of hiking, biking, and equestrian trails wind through wooded canyons and along hidden coves. To the north, rugged, untamed coastline, mostly the domain of the giant Hearst Corporation, remains a remnant of the natural splendor that greeted early explorers of California.

I exited at Los Osos Valley Road just before the off ramp for Morro Bay and found myself in the middle of Steinbeck Country. Tidy rows of vegetables fan to the road from turn-of-the-century farmhouses.

The rich smell of freshly cut hay filled the air as a lone farmer on his tractor tilled the earth. This road delivered me to the entrance of Montana de Oro. Pecho Valley Road marks the beginning of an eleven-mile drive through shady eucalyptus groves atop rugged bluffs overlooking a four-mile sand spit; part of the Morro Dunes Nature Preserve. In the distance, 575-foot Morro Rock, the smallest of nine volcanic outcroppings in the region, stands as sentinel to the entrance of Morro Bay.

Spirits soared when I reached Spooner Cove, a strip of sand scalloped into the cliffs at the end of the road. I couldn't wait to hike the bluff trail to the south of the cove and suck in the brisk sea air. The trail meanders along the edge of the sea cliffs overlooking white mountains of water crashing against the sea wall. From this vantage, I spied oystercatchers sleeping in the sun, pelicans flying low in V-formation scouting for fish broils, and sea ducks with bright red feet dunking for tidbits.

The two-mile beach trail connects with Coon Creek Trail, an *Alice in Wonderland* tree tunnel that beckons the hiker to enter. The tree-shaded trail laced with cucumber vines and wildflowers, traces the course of a trickling stream. It is an easy march into this lush fairyland of cool ferns and mosses. Complete trail maps are available at Park Headquarters located in the original Spooner ranch house under a lone stand of wind-bent cypress overlooking Spooner Cove. Overnight campsites are available.

South Bay Boulevard off Los Osos Valley Road takes you through the famed Morro Bay Estuary, past the state park camping grounds, and through the back door to Morro Bay. Audubon Club members flock here to see the thousands of migratory birds that blacken the skies each February. In June, the rust-colored meadow is sprinkled with snowy egret and redwing blackbirds. An immature green heron standing in the marsh doing his imitation of a stick almost fooled me. There is a natural history museum in the park filled with a fine collection of Chumash Indian relics.

North of the museum, across from the golf course, is the largest heron rookery on the West Coast. The mating birds clustered here make a great racket with their beaks that sounds like someone slapping bamboo sticks together. High overhead, huge nests of the great egret can be seen in the eucalyptus trees. I watched the large white birds regurgitate fish into the waiting beaks of their feisty offspring. Great blue herons nest here as well as hundreds of cormorants and the night green heron.

Scanning the back bay below the rookery with my binoculars, I spotted a flotilla of white pelican in the distance. A local woman was setting up her painting easel a few feet away from me.

"Want to see some white pelicans?" I asked.

"Those are egrets," she said. "Lived here since 1960. Never heard of white pelican." She huffed, turning back to her work. I handed her my glasses.

"I'll be! They ARE white pelicans! Who'd believe an "out-of-towner" could show me something new about this place." The birds floated in unison toward us giving us a close-up look at their ghostly white feathers and yellow beaks.

There is a fierce competition among local restaurants for the best seafood dishes to win the tourist dollar. Each night I enjoyed a sensational entry to the contest. At the Galley, a family-owned establishment, one of the oldest restaurants on the wharf, I sampled razorback clams sautéed in a garlic wine sauce. At Rosie's, just down the boardwalk, I dined on their outdoor patio and tried the "all you can eat" seafood special. The service is slow in summer, but the fresh Dungeness crab is worth the wait.

All restaurants, including Dorn's, a breakfast hotspot sport views of the bay and the fishing boats cutting V-shaped trails across the placid water. Morro Rock, populated by nesting seagulls and the occasional peregrine falcon, watches over the bay. Shorebirds of all sorts flit through the skies. A frisky sea otter floated by my window. He scratched his belly with wild abandon until he was so tickled with himself he had to do about twenty revolutions in the water to relax.

The otter has had a rough time surviving. At the turn of the century, Russians imported the Aleut to hunt them along the coast of California. In our lifetime, fishing boats with long lines and nets have taken their toll on their numbers. But in Morro Bay, otters are enjoying a comeback. In fact, there are too many otters (according to the owner-operator of the sub-sea boat that offers tours of the harbor daily). "They are hungry all the time," he said. "They have huge appetites." Between the otter and human consumption, there are no abalone left in the bay. A mother otter slipped by floating on her back tapping a mussel on a rock she'd placed on her belly. Her four-month old kit trailed in her wake. The quizzical expression on the kit's whiskery face made me glad the otters are ahead this inning.

Next day, I headed north: Destination, Salmon Creek State Park just above the San Luis Obispo county line. I stopped at Piedras Blancas on Highway One, four miles north of San Simeon and Hearst Castle. Tourists were lined up overlooking the sandy beach. Elephant seals congregate here in spring and early summer to fast and molt their top layer of fat. One might lift its head to make a noise that sounds like a snore through a lead pipe from the bottom of the well, but that's all the action you will see the rest of the year. In February, you can witness the fierce battles between 12-foot males weighing in at 6,000 pounds for the privilege of mating with one of the temptresses sprawled on the sand. It's tough being an alpha male in this tribe. It's so stressful fending off the young Turks while keeping around twenty-five females happy at the same time, that they only last a couple seasons. Good grounds for monogamy.

From there, I drove past the Piedras Blancas Lighthouse built in 1875 to watch over this rugged stretch of untrammeled coastline. The surf is rough at these beaches, so don't swim alone. The tide pooling and hiking are grand. I found Salmon Creek State Park just beyond Ragged Point, the last vantage point in San Lois Obispo County on the Pacific Coast Highway. The trailhead, with parking for four cars, is nestled in one of the many horseshoe curves of Highway One. A weathered wooden gate opens into an enchanted forest of ferns, blackberry vines, and towering sycamores. The path has a steep grade and eventually takes the more intrepid hiker to a sixty-foot waterfall. I settled for a half-mile Big Sur sampler, stopping long enough to soak in the magnificent vista of the electric blue Pacific far below.

On the way back to Morro Bay, a stop at Cayucos, a laid-back western beach town was in order. I melted into the comfy patio furniture on the deck of Schooner's restaurant, protected from the wind by a glass shield with a view of the fishermen on the pier and surfers plying the waves. I ordered steamed clams in a scrumptious butter, wine, mushroom, and shallot concoction along with the house salad of greens topped with a tangy raspberry poppy seed dressing. The Schooner won the seafood contest, hands down. I patted a contented belly. The end of a successful sojourn into Central California just three hours from L.A. had arrived and it was time to go home.

Wet, Wild, and Wonderful - Patagonia

I am sipping coffee at Hotel Lago Grey in Torres del Paine, Chile before everyone arrives for breakfast. An exquisite rainbow is arcing to the left of a panorama of turquoise glacier-fed waters framed in snow-tipped-giants that soar to 10,000 feet. I feel as misty as the gauzy clouds drifting over the Paine Massif; privileged to behold the grandeur before me.

The five-hour drive across the undulating plains of Patagonia Steppe from Punta Arenas to Torres del Paine garnered many wildlife sightings. The lesser rhea, a bird in the ostrich family, and the favorite food of the Tehuelche Indians was our first encounter. The crested caracara, an opportunist by nature who stays close to the roadside hoping for easy pickings, became a common sighting. A highlight was watching an awkward takeoff by a grounded condor flapping his 9-foot wing span. We spotted a lone gaucho trotting briskly across the tawny waves of billowing grasses. They are as rare as a puma sighting since the sheep industry gave way to tourism in the region.

We passed Puerto Nogales where our local guide, Kris, lives in a house with no electricity or running water. She carts in water and has a generator and wood-burning stove for heat. Her life is rugged and hard, but she says she finds freedom in her walks in the mountains. She feels safe there. No snakes, no mosquitos, no altitude sickness, nothing that could harm a human save the elements that she knows how to read and is prepared for. She leads trekkers from around the globe who come to explore the magical vales on 5 and 10-day circuits in the park.

I fell in step behind Kris as we leaned into the wind on our first hike. It was into a lonely valley with a clear view of the salmon-colored towers of the

Torres del Paine that pulled me to the ends of the earth an 8-hour hike away. This Guanaco trail was lined with humps of a prickly bush only the guanaco can eat with their sticky tongues. Guanaco, distant relatives of the llama with doe eyes and gentle demeanor, will spit a vile green slime on you if you get too close They provided the Tehuelche with fur for their capes, foot coverings, and tents along with meat that they ate raw.

At Hotel Lago Grey, lodging inside the park, travelers congregate in the lounge with its warm ambiance and walls of glass overlooking Lago Grey. Once bedded down, I listened to a rowdy wind tossing the tree canopy and rain pelting my window. I slept like a squirrel with his tail tucked over his head and woke to the sun streaming through the mist rising on the emerald green grass.

Mood swings in the weather are the norm. Layered clothing is the order of the day with rain pants in your daypack for good measure. We determined to stroll through the forest on the shore of Grey Lago to a swinging bridge across an energetic river to a view of the snout of the Grey Glacier. The path is lined with shrubs with tiny red berries locals turn into jam. There are yellow orchids, sweet peas, and fungi in the mossy undergrowth. The beech tree or linga draped with old man's beard, and the monkey puzzle is the most common trees. A solo stroll in the sheltered forest back to the lodge listening to birdsong made me very happy in that moment.

Furious winds lifting the waters to a cooling spray greeted us at Salto Grande, a turgid, turquoise waterfall charging from Lago Nordenskjold into Lago Pehoe. On our afternoon hike to the base of the famous Cuernos del Paine, aka the Horns, Kris taught us to spot water mists dancing on the metallic lake. They tell you that a blast of air strong enough to knock a man off his feet is on the way. You learn to look for a protected area behind green mounds, and if you can't find it you turn your back to the wind and place one foot in front of you and take a stand. The winds have blasted bowls of granite into the imposing mountain and carved shafts into sharp fingers piercing blue skies. Ominous lenticular clouds crowding overhead fanned across the heavens. They can turn mean in moments and let loose a downpour that may pass as fast as it comes, but we were graced with a crystalline day.

As I look out over Grey Lago stippled with white caps and see the leaves whipping wildly in the cease-less wind, I feel lucky to be here and to experience some of the Creator's most magnificent handiwork. It is the grandeur and the awful power of the craggy giants reaching for the heavens guarding Grey Lago that remind me that wet and wild places are worth saving.

Sinking into River Time

Every bend of the river beckons—
every pool may bring better luck.
Life should be like that.
—Zane Grey

The Rogue River is a vital artery in southern Oregon that flows 215 miles from Crater Lake to Gold Beach on the coast. Rainie Falls is the take-out point for rafters to the 40-mile stretch of the wild and scenic corridor on the infamous Rogue. We skirted this big drop into a gaping hole, the only Class 4 rapid through the preserved wilderness to Agnes we encountered. We listened for the rumble of rapids ahead as we coasted on jade-green waters beneath cerulean skies watching eagles and turkey vultures soar overhead. Several blue heron fishing on the shore fly-hopped ahead of us on our way down the river to our first camp.

Momentum River Expeditions takes pride in letting travelers be part of the adventure. You can row

147

as much as you choose, or not row at all. It is your holiday. If you want to man your own boat, you can float in the rubber ducky (inflatable kayak), jump into the clear water to cool off, and swim beside the boat during calm glides. Or you can sit back, do a little birding, and watch the world go by. At the end of a rafting day, you will be greeted by your camp guide with tents popped, a latrine installed, and cool lemonade. While you settle into your home for the night, your guides, like elves in the forest, prepare tasty, creative appetizers, and ply you with fine Oregon wines. Dinners are delicious creations from chicken with ginger sauce to steak spiked with chimichurri. Fresh vegetables from farm to table magically appear. Leave room for dessert.

Mornings are cool and serene with the sun casting a golden shine on translucent waters so clear you can see the polished rocks below. Ospreys, with their nests in the sugar pines sheathing the canyon walls, circle overhead. A strategic dive garners a fishy breakfast. Flocks of Canada geese in V-formation squawk at their neighbors as they fly up the canyon. Troops of goslings and mergansers float near the river-banks and hide in the foliage on shore. A doe entered our camp at happy hour with two spotted fawns in tow. When we left our last camp, a black bear ambled along the shore as if to say farewell to humans in its domain.

A shady hike up Whiskey Creek brought us to the remains of a cabin where an enterprising back-to-the-lander lived in self-contained isolation. My favorite stop was a pleasant stroll through a vast and manicured meadow at the Rogue River Ranch that led to a deep swimming hole. A flashy orange building houses a museum that is left open for visitors to explore. We stopped at Zane Grey's cabin where he enjoyed solitude as he described so lovingly in his book *Feud on the Rogue River*. He was a fishing fool, and loved this region where salmon and steelhead trout abound.

Mule Creek Canyon is a deep, narrow gorge framed in craggy rocks sculpted into magical formations. Boulders softened by the incessant flow are scooped out with holes that looked like eyes peering down upon us. We stopped at an icy cascade tumbling over a rock ledge to fill our water jugs. A white line on the bank of the river three feet above the water line marked the water level just three weeks ago. At this time of year (July), in the middle of a heat wave and drought, the river is less energetic and easier to manage. In the spring it can be a raging inferno bouncing rafters off the walls through this chute.

Each bend in the river indeed brought us something new. Our comforts were well taken care of and all that was required of us was to enjoy the river corridor with its abundant wildlife and rich history of gold miners, fishermen, Native Americans, and river rats of all stripes.

The Rogue River Trail overlooks the river and traces the path of the rafters. In spring, Momentum offers a raft-hike option for the hardier. They set up camp and prepare meals for hikers who want to enjoy trekking with a daypack and looking forward to their comforts being provided at the end of their hiking day. There is also the option of a lodge-to-lodge rafting trip that runs simultaneously with the camp trip, so those who prefer the conveniences of the lodge can have the same rafting experience as the rest of the people in their party. There are options for all levels of physical fitness and desire for adventure. This is a wonderful opportunity for families to share. Children are welcome with a parent or guardian. The trip promises to make kids braver and make adults kids again.

I loved manning the ducky through riffles, splashing through rapids, and spinning onto a serene glide. I learned how to read the river following the bubble line, avoid getting sucked into eddies, and paddling hard against the headwind that comes up in the afternoon. Unlike my guides and other guests, I wasn't into jumping off rock ledges into deep pools in the river. I relished a moment beneath a swaying canopy of birch beside a giggling creek while the rest of the crew hiked to a water slide. The lushness of the spreading ferns and moss-covered trees blessed with a soft breeze off the water gave me time to breathe in the cool beauty of the forest and let me sink into river time.

Waterfall Wonderland
Columbia River Gorge and
the Mt. Hood River Valley-Oregon

Elowah Falls in Oregon's Columbia River Gorge cascades in endless curtains of white. I sat mesmerized in the cooling mist and relished the sight of it being whipped sideways by a wild wind. While I could have lingered in this amphitheater of yellow lichen and green moss, there was far more to see so I had to get moving. The hike continues on a narrow ledge overlooking the impressive Columbia River dotted with islands. Lewis and Clark's Corp of Discovery was known to have camped on one of them directly below.

The muscular Columbia River flows more than 1,200 miles from the base of the Canadian Rockies to the coast of Oregon. Today it is dammed in eleven places making it a tamed house cat compared to the raging torrent it was when early explorers arrived. The Columbia River Gorge was declared a national scenic area in 1986 and spans 292,000 acres of wildness. Train rails on both sides of the river transport goods from the interior to the coast, and Highway 84 on the Oregon side is a busy thorough-fare with access to numerous foot trails leading to over forty waterfalls. Yes, you can read one of the numerous hiking guidebooks for the region, but having a seasoned guide who has tried them all and knows the special treats in store on each one is a wonderful thing.

Our shakedown run took us up the canyon through towering Douglas fir and stands of alder. The song of the well-hidden feathered set kept us company on the ascent overlooking a creek carving a path through luxuriant foliage. Tender meadow rue and the sweet white blooms of miner's lettuce and trillium lined the path. In the distance, the rumble of a great fall pulled us onward and upward over sometimes rocky terrain. The lush coolness of the forest glens soothed and refreshed. I loved hiking in the deepening silence of the trees and away from the rushing traffic falling behind us.

The mean age of our group of twelve was about 50. Most of these experienced hikers were travelers who hiked in various locations around the U.S. and Europe. This is not a competitive event. "Easy-peasy" options are given at the onset of each outing. I scored about a five on the one-to-ten fitness scale in our group of hikers, preferring to dawdle behind taking snaps and smelling the profusion of wild blooms. One of the guests, a young man from Phoenix who was used to climbing in the slot canyons of Arizona, wanted to experience Oneonta Gorge which required swimming—yes swimming!—to reach the base of a thundering cascade. A special outing was arranged for him so he would not go home disappointed.

After a day of exploring, we crossed over the Bridge of the Gods to the Washington side of the Columbia to our digs overlooking the Cascade Range. Stately Skamania Lodge boasts gourmet cuisine, zip lines, an 18-hole golf course, and four miles of hiking trails. I couldn't wait to slip into the outdoor spa and listen to the wind stirring the trees under pure blue skies. With the tension melted from my body followed by a swim in the Olympic-sized pool, I felt born again.

No trip to the Gorge is complete without a hike up popular Eagle Creek. The moment you enter the well-groomed path, you are swallowed in green. Chatty smaller streams join the run through the majestic forest. The drop-off naturally becomes more precipitous as you climb up the canyon. Often the trail narrows to a ledge with a well-placed handrail to steady your nerves. Sprays of pink and white flowers nestled in ferns cling to the basalt canyon walls, and around each bend is another stunning view of the deepening chasm. Devil's Punchbowl is the first of three falls along the way to High Bridge, our lunch destination. Rock walls deep in the canyon are matted with mosses, ferns, and lichens. With abundant life all about, I felt refreshed, soothed, restored, and deliriously happy to be here. Four miles in, we crossed over a heart-catching cleft in basalt walls with black water flowing far below. At our lunch stop, I shed my boots and dangled my dogs in the tingling water while our guides laid out a delicious spread.

Not to be outdone by the beauty of the Gorge, Washington's majestic, white-capped Mt. Hood towers over nearby Hood River Valley. A serene walk around Lost Lake garnered a shot of the icon reflected in still waters. While other hikers did the more dramatic Lost Lake Butte hike with even more stunning panoramas, I fended off scrappy chipmunks threatening to invade our picnic table.

Before heading back to civilization, a brisk walk along the banks of the rushing Salmon River was the order of the day. We could see the rocks on the bottom of the clear river where rainbow trout lurked. It was raining in earnest on this walk, but the canopy of the old-growth forest took the brunt of the weather. The limbs of the monster trees sheathed in moss and draped in old man's beard are twisted into alien forms. We puddle-jumped up the soggy trail and got quite lost in the fecund smells of this wet world. It is an undulating track that leaves your mind free to wonder at the bizarre formations of the trees and makes you glad to know they have been spared the logger's axe. The trees were witness to the Native peoples fishing for salmon on the shores of these bountiful waters, and the early explorers and homesteaders who struggled to survive the Oregon Trail to make this place their home. Happily, they are with us still and can be enjoyed by moderns wanting to reconnect with nature and their primal yearnings.

Romp Across the Top of the World - Ecuador

Have you ever dreamed of galloping across the top of the world beneath the bluest of skies plumped with billowing clouds? Imagine green and gold spires poking through those clouds and a wild wind whipping your spirits as you canter on with a racing heart. Now, breathe in crystalline air as you fall in sync with the rhythm of your horse's hoof beat, and let your mind go sailing. Thanks to Sally Vergette, this ride is waiting for you in the northern highlands of the Andes in Ecuador. Possessed of sparkling energy and deep love for the horses she provides, Sally loves sharing the less traveled "paremo" the unique Andean grasslands of the high country.

The journey from hacienda to hacienda along the slopes of the sacred Imbabura Volcano begins in the Otavalo valley, one the last strongholds of Indigenous peoples famous for their weaving skills. Our group of nine equestriennes stopped at the Otavalo Marketplace where we bargained for ponchos and scarves for the ride. The scent of pigs roasting and the colorful displays of handcrafted goods, not to mention bargain prices, made for an exciting bazaar.

We spent the first night at Hacienda Pensaqui, an oasis nestled among humble villages. There we enjoyed a delicious meal and local Andean musicians. Chambermaids lit warming fires in our rooms, turned down our comfy beds, and slipped a hot water bottle between the sheets for good measure.

In 1540 Spanish conquistadors came to this land of extremes in search of gold. With just 2,000 soldiers they conquered the Incas and Native tribes living in the tranquil valleys framed by majestic volcanic peaks. The conquerors were granted huge plots of land by the Spanish crown. Lavish haciendas with elaborate gardens, elegant furnishings, paintings, sculptures, and murals sprang up across the land. After 300 years of tyrannical rule, the Spanish were ousted and

Ecuador claimed its independence. Today these haciendas are being restored and serve as gracious quarters for travelers.

Our first day of riding began on a narrow track overlooking a gulch lined with eucalyptus trees. We climbed ever higher until we could see Lake Pablo glistening in the distance. Soon we were greeted by Santiago and his charming wife at their ranch overlooking the valley far below. Santiago led our band of merry ladies up still higher on a track he had cleared in the primarily untouched highland forest behind his home. The clip of hummingbirds diving into dangling blooms of bright red penstemon was all that could be heard. A profusion of yellow blooms crowned the arnica trees and purple lupine decorated the lush green tree tunnel of mountain bamboo.

We cantered on to even higher ground where the troubles of the world melted away like lemon drops. Thick fleece saddle covers kept us comfortable riding for six hours. By five o'clock we were trotting along cobblestone lanes through another village to our quarters at Hacienda Cusin where we gathered by a fire burning in the cozy den. A three-course meal was served on a table graced with roses and fine china, and the evening was spent in gentle conversation of a time gone by.

I awoke to sunlight streaming through my window and looked out at gardens bursting with blooms.

Linda Ballou

The horses were tacked and ready. "Hola!" called smiling children waving from rooftops as our procession passed through their village. We rode through manicured plots of green, purple, and gold that created a patchwork quilt nearly covering the mountainsides. Pigs, sheep, and cattle grazed along the way, and committees of barking dogs charging out to guard their territory became commonplace. Once back on the high ground, we cantered through undulating fields of wheat glowing in the buttery sun.

We descended on a narrow heart-thumping trail through the colorful tapestry of industrious people leading simple lives close to the land. A mist hit us, followed by a few drops of rain, and then a rainbow arced over the pastoral scene. At the end of this spectacular day we rode through the gates of La Merced nestled in the cleft of a mountain sheathed in pine. Prize-winning Andalusian horses munching on knee-high grass let us know we were close to Spain in spirit. After a ride over the ranchlands with views of three peaks in Columbia, a fun romp through a pungent eucalyptus forest brought us home.

For this intermediate ride, you must be able to ride at all gaits and be in control of your mount at all times. Our group was comprised of seasoned riders except for one athletic woman who had taken riding lessons for six months. Sally offers shorter rides for families and less experienced riders. This four-day ride from hacienda to hacienda can be done in conjunction with a three-day trek on the flank of Cotopaxi, the highest volcano in Ecuador. That stretch provides a tremendously thrilling ride across wild, sometimes desolate terrain, with striking views of the snow-capped volcano. Since she began organizing rides in Ecuador in 1996, Sally has branched out to guide rides in the mountains of Brazil, Chile, and Uruguay.

If you go, plan to spend a night in Quito to adjust to the altitude and enjoy touring Old Town.

Glacier Bay - Wildlife Haven

We flew close to the barren rock peaks that support no visible life. They are copper colored, not black as they appear when looking at them from the distant ground. I spied a moose marsh—a happy spot for beaver, martin, and more. Wings is considered one of the safest, best-maintained small airlines in southeast Alaska, but my stomach is churning. I'm anxious to land and get to Glacier Bay where thirteen tidewater glaciers converge; it's a landscape on the move and declared a World Heritage site.

The morning sun casting pink light across the south face of the mountains promises an unforgettable day. In half an hour, we approach Gustavus Airport. A dense mist covers the valley like steam over a witch's cauldron. Our pilot descends from crystalline skies into the fog bank and makes a masterful landing. There are no roads to this remote paradise, only small planes or a daily ferry from Juneau can bring you here. The shuttle van from Glacier Bay Lodge is waiting.

The driver makes a beeline through a tree tunnel

of stunted spruce. It is a young forest—only 200 years old. Verdant and strong. Gustavus is the jumping-off point for boats and planes entering Glacier Bay. It boasts miles of sandy beach which is unique to the region. Shaggy cows and ponies graze in pastures of billowing knee-high grass. There are 250 year-round residents. The population bulges to 1,000 during May through mid-September, considered the summer season. We speed by the Gustavus Inn, a cozy bed and breakfast that provides bicycles for those who chose to pedal to the 3.3 million-acre national park ten miles away.

The driver pulls into the lodge and whisks my luggage to my room. I enter the lodge with its open cathedral beams, warming fire, and a wall of glass overlooking the boat harbor. There is a comfortable viewing deck where guests may have a drink or dine. All that can be heard is the soothing breath of the forest and the squawk of an occasional seagull. I fuel up on a lumberjack buffet breakfast. Fortified for a day brimming with sunshine, I march down the path to the dock where the *Spirit of Adventure* is waiting.

I lean up the ramp of the 150-passenger catamaran—the best way to see the bay. John Muir explored the fiords of Glacier Bay in 1879 in a 60-foot spruce canoe with a Tlingit Indian guide. I'm glad to have two glass-enclosed decks to roam and an open deck on top for viewing. Our captain, an energetic young woman with a ponytail down to her waist, wears a crisp naval white and blue uniform. Introduction to the cruise by the ship's naturalist, a park ranger, is interrupted by the sighting of a sow with two cubs. While scanning the shore with field glasses looking for the bears, I spy a sea otter floating close by the boat showing off the kit she carries on her belly.

Surf scoters darken the sky as they lift in the thousands before the bow of the boat cutting through metallic water. Flocks of black oystercatchers joining them create an excited fluttery curtain. We cruise close to South Marble Island, home to the tufted and horned puffin. They work hard to fly, beating short wings in the air, but in the water, they dive hundreds of feet effortlessly. Jaunty fellows in black tuxedos, seem overdressed for the occasion. They share this tiny rock island with nesting kittiwake gulls, pigeon guillemot, and murres. Stellar sea lions, thousand-pound mountains of flesh, hoist themselves onto the north tip of the island to roar at the day. The males are territorially bound during the breeding season, while the females are free spirits that come and go at will. It's one more group where "women are smarter."

Mountain goats watch us from their rocky ledge. The cruise ships plying the fiords to the glacier snouts are their daily amusement. The lazy day brings a bear out to sleep in the sun beside a boulder. He lifts his head taking notice of us then goes back to snoozing.

Linda Ballou

Though the sun is high overhead the air temp is about 60 and the windchill factor from the moving boat puts it at about 40 degrees. Roxanne, a young woman from Ottawa, where it often gets 50 below, is in her element. She spread her arms wide embracing the day. "I feel invigorated, fresh, and alive," she cries. I am warmed by her enthusiasm, but my teeth still chatter. I don't want to leave the breezy viewing deck, so I hug myself and suppress thoughts about the fleece pants I left behind in a drawer in Southern California.

The ranger announces that we are entering John Hopkins Inlet, the "jawbreaker" of the journey. We make a hard left turn and enter the womb of all time. The sheer rock walls jutting up on either side of the cove are scraped clean by the retreating glacier. Our captain slyly maneuvers through the bergs that create a chunky brew fanning two miles in front of the great ice river. I hear them crunching against our hull. The glacier is spawned in the Fairweather Range, a staggering fortress of jagged teeth reaching heights of 16,000 feet. The artist is still at work here sculpting snow castles in lapis lazuli skies. The spirits of the ancient Tlingit who lived here 10,000 years ago are released from their frozen tombs with an unearthly howl and claps of thunder when enormous chunks of ice calve from the glacier. It is a joyous bursting forth from the ice. Crystal creations shaped like birds, fish, and men melt in the dazzling sun. The water broils beneath them until they dissipate into the milky green, disappearing into the still air.

I spot two kayakers—brave souls I consider to be part of the wildlife in Glacier Bay. They nose close to the foot of John Hopkins Glacier. If they should tip over and are unable to perform an Eskimo roll successfully, they are guaranteed a heart attack within three minutes of hitting the water. They are close enough to the glacier to see the over 6,000 harbor seals hauled out onto the icebergs. Safe from orca, the killer whale, the seals give birth to their young on floating fortresses. Newborns can swim almost immediately from birth. Disturbance of the bond between mother and pup in the first week or so after birth can lead to permanent abandonment of the pup. For this reason, John Hopkins Inlet is closed beyond Jaw Point to all boats from May 1 to June 30.

The boat has stopped so we may listen without the interference of engine noise. Guests crowded on the viewing deck include a couple from Holland, a folksy couple from Texas doing a video for RV enthusiasts, and two young men from Switzerland. I ask the men if the snow-drenched mountains behind the glacier rival the Matterhorn in beauty. "There is no contest. The immenseness of the northwest overshadows the Alps," they say without hesitation. We hover in the inlet hoping for a calving of ice telling us we are in the Bay of Thunder. Mother Nature, however, is not cooperating. I must rely on John Muir to describe the phenomenon.

"Passengers were happy, gazing at the beautiful blue of the bergs and the shattered pinnacled crystal wall, awed by the thunder and commotion of the falling and rising icebergs, whichever and anon sent spray flying several hundred feet into the air and raised swells that set all the fleet of bergs in motion and roared up the beach, telling the story of the birth of every iceberg far and near." *Travels in Alaska*, John Muir.

On the return leg of the journey, we cruise close to the face of Marjorie Glacier. I see cerulean caverns glowing from the depths of the crystal columns jutting into the sky. The dripping from the glass castle melting in the warm sun sounds like a pipe organ playing an eerie tune. After soaking in the height, breadth, and depth of the kaleidoscopic face of the glacier, we head back to the lodge.

Guests sharing the warming fire with me include a pair of backpackers getting a mainline of protein in the form of a Berg Berger after a week of granola bars and freeze-dried dinners; two young women planning to take advantage of kayaks for hire in Bartlett Cove the next day; and a couple from Redondo in the middle of their quest for the perfect retirement spot. It is September, the tail end of the season; the rangers are toasting one another goodbye. Soon they will be departing to warmer summer quarters like the thousands of migratory birds that come here each year to nest. After a splendid version of seafood linguini prepared with the local clams, mussels, and crab, I turn in early.

I awake to the thump of pinecones on the roof. Lazy in a warm bed in my open-beam cottage, I'm tempted to sleep until noon. That, however, is the scheduled departure time for the Auk Nu, a catamaran that takes travelers up Icy Straights on a half day whale-watching cruise and doubles as the ferry service to Juneau. With this adventure in mind, I jump up and spread the blinds to a brilliant day. It only shines about 45 days out of the year in Glacier Bay aka "Land of Ocean Mists," but when it does, the day will not let you rest. I stuff a rain slicker into my day-pack knowing that in Alaska the weather can be moody.

A van shuttle takes me to the Gustavus dock where I board the Auk Nu. We chug into a headwind toward the whale feeding grounds. Leicester Island rests like a sleeping crocodile on the horizon. A haze softens the tender blue sky to a muted pastel water-color painting. The Fairweather Range looks like a dreamy snow fortress in the distance. They appear so soft I imagine I could fall from the sky and land on them unharmed. Rounded humps of green a mere ten thousand feet up are at the fore of this picture.

The captain spots the spouts of a pod of the

humpback whale. He accelerates and we are on the trail. I saw humpback earlier this year in Baja. They migrate from Hawaii and Baja, California to the bay each year. I wonder if one of the four whales we are following shared the warmer waters with me. Humpbacks don't feed year-round; they spend four to seven months gorging on krill, shrimp, and schools of fish. They work together to create what is known as a bubble net. One or more whales dive under a school of fish and swim in a circle casting a net of bubbles around the fish from their blowholes. Then they lunge up through the bubble net collecting the confused fish in massive jaws.

There is a raft of kayakers precariously close to the 35-ton creatures we are following at a safe distance. The paddlers tap on the bottom of their boats letting the giants know they are there. The whales sensitive to sound are supposed to be smart enough to avoid them. I don't think these adventurers have read the same story I did about a veteran kayaker lifted out of the water when she was caught in a whale bubble net.

Four energetic whales spout rhythmically, blowing six-foot sprays of water into the air as they wend their way up the channel. They arc their 50-foot length, curling great gray backs into the water, proudly lifting their tails for all to see. Scientists can tell the whales apart by battle scars and other distinguishing features on their tails. One female we are following has a distinctive foghorn blow attributed to a deviated septum. Although the whales are enjoying a comeback from near extinction, their population is estimated to be 1,200 in the North Pacific. Fifteen to thirty-five feed seasonally in the bay waters. Studies are presently underway to determine if the noise from the cruise traffic is harming their numbers.

We are approaching a narrow channel where the Pacific Ocean converges with the headwaters of Glacier Bay and Icy Straights creating a raging tidal river. The captain slows to a few knots while navigating the treacherous chop. The tidal action churns plankton and krill to the surface making it a popular feeding area for all marine mammals. I see the fin of a giddy Steller sea lion. He does acrobatic swirls making circles with his flippers in the air while he cleans up after the whales. Four jaegers swoop down on the seagulls making off with the fish in their beaks. These predatory birds badger other birds until they drop their catch then scoop it up for themselves. A sea otter back-paddles past our bow, curling under just before disaster.

We leave the whales and cruise between a small island and the shore. Out of the wind, we patrolled the shore in search of Sitka deer. One small meadow, damp with dew glistening in the sun, is populated by the tents of independent kayakers. We pass harbor seals recharging their batteries on the rocks. About ten lay in a lumpy tan-colored heap at the edge of the velvet green spruce and hemlock forest. The sun high overhead does fandangles on the jade-green water holding nothing back. Soft white clouds are smeared across the baby blue sky, and it is calm. So calm, I melt into the scenery as I soak in the lazy day.

Parting Thought

Nature Can Be Our Salvation

I am not an atheist but an earthiest. Be true to the earth.
—Edward Abbey

Earthiests are those who literally need to plug into the planet to recharge. I am one among them. Whether sitting on a sun-warmed rock, face planted down on a sandy beach, atop a mountain with arms spread and palms up, or resting against a tree, I am gathering energy from the earth.

Some people think nothing is happening when they are sitting still because their minds are too busy to feel anything. But they are receiving nature's gift just the same. An earthiest consciously makes themselves more receptive to the bounty by quieting their minds and will not miss an opportunity to plug into the universal charging station.

Henry David Thoreau, our nation's first self-proclaimed nature nut, walked four hours each day. He sauntered through the woods and over the hills and fields of New England so that his thoughts were "absolutely free from all worldly engagements." My walks allow me time to digest the constant stimulation of urban life and the opportunity to reflect and recycle thoughts in a format that is hopefully satisfying to readers.

My connection with Mother Earth began in my teenage years in southeastern Alaska. Lonely walks along misty shores allowed tumultuous adolescent thoughts to settle. According to an anonymous source who etched the following into a cliff wall at Anza Borrego Desert, "Solitude is not something you hope for in the future. It allows a deepening of the present and without it you will never find it." The desert landscape supports this theory. From a distance it looks barren, but as you come closer and examine it in silence, you see creatures scurry at your footfall and plants spring to life from parched soil.

None of this is new. Through nature, the Navajo strive to achieve Hózhó, a harmony and balance within themselves and their society. Ancient Hawaiians lifted their fingertips to the sky in hula to pull mana or spiritual energy into their being. They received powerful energy from *moana*, the grand and vibrant sea. The practice of simply being calm and quiet among the trees, observing nature and breathing deeply is called "forest bathing." This ancient Japanese process is gaining popularity around the world today. Moderns are practicing "earthing" which is walking barefoot to balance again with natural forces and counteract the effects of exposure to electro-magnetic fields from our phones and other devices.

I find sustenance and solace in nature. My daily walks are a meditation. They allow my mind to relax and wander freely. Earbuds and distracting devices are left behind. I want to be fully present to hear the birds twittering and the wind whispering through the trees. Subconscious thoughts have space and time to bubble up to the surface. I want to digest all the input I receive each day. My overstimulated molecules settle into place, and I find answers to my questions in my writing and in life this way.

Nature can be our salvation. It is for me.

Thank You to My Hosts

Many of the wonderful adventures I share in this collection were made possible by various hosts. A SPECIAL THANKS goes to Overseas Adventure Travel which is geared to the over 55 traveler. The journey with them through Africa took me on safari in Botswana, Zimbabwe, and Zambia. This trip remains at the top of the incredible adventures I've taken that I could not have pulled off by myself. Torres del Paine in the southern tip of Chile, another fantastic destination that I wouldn't dare to attempt to maneuver alone, was arranged by OAT. In between Buenos Aires to Patagonia there were many wonders I would have missed out on without their expert guidance. My last journey with OAT was an expansive tour of Australia from Melbourne to the Daintree Rainforest in the northwest with stops in the interior on the way. Australia is a huge country that requires interior flights and a deep knowledge of its terrain and microclimates to enjoy your explorations. Momentum River Expeditions let me join the company rafting the

Rogue River in Oregon during the pandemic when I desperately needed to be outdoors. Rafting the Grand Canyon is a life-changing journey that I treasure. I am forever grateful to Grand Canyon Expeditions for letting me experience the marvels waiting for travelers at the bottom of the grandest canyon of them all. Active New Zealand was one of the first companies to host me. The mystical beauty of the South Island remains a favorite in all my travels.

The one person I really must thank is Anne Holmes, "Boomer in Chief" at the National Association of Baby Boomer Women. I am the Adventure Travel Expert on the site. She makes my work look good and has given me my own column that is syndicated to 89 family magazines throughout the U.S. This provides me a bull horn for my hosts and guarantees that I will be able to get the word out about their offerings.

I look forward to more exciting journeys. Like Victorian Age explorer Isabella Bird, I am fully engaged in the state of exploration. I must give a nod here to my pioneering parents who are no longer with us. Being uprooted at the tender age of 13 and transplanted in a tiny town in southeast Alaska was a head-spinning event that changed me forever. I must thank them for introducing me to the majesty of the wilds that captivate me and give me the courage to follow my "bear heart."

If you are interested in becoming a travel writer,

check out *Get Great Trips for Free* available in the Kindle store on Amazon. In it, I share the renegade way to get trips that has worked for me.

Meet the Author

Linda Ballou is an award-winning travel writer and author of three novels. "Bright Blossom in the Pacific" and "On the Road with the Lady of the Rockies" were both Solas winners at Travel Tales Publications. Her articles have appeared in numerous national magazines and e-zines. An avid horsewoman, her first articles were in horse-centric magazines like Equus and *Horse Illustrated*. She has taken horse treks in Ireland, Ecuador, British Columbia, and many parts of the Wild West. Her second favorite mode of transport is a rubber raft. If that is not available, there are always hiking boots.

Lost Angel in Paradise is 32 day trips up her beloved coast of California from Malibu to Mendocino. She takes you on a moderate hike, inserts historical tidbits, and ends a beautiful day at an outdoor eatery.

Lost Angel Walkabout won the Bronze Award given by the National Association of Travel Journalists. It received praise from other notable travel writers like Rolf Potts of Vagabonding fame and

James Dorsey, intrepid traveler, and award-winning author.

"*Lost Angel Walkabout* by Linda Ballou takes the reader out of their armchair and into the vast world as few travel writers can. Her eye for detail combined with intimate knowledge of her surroundings sets Ms. Ballou heads above most of the travel writing pack. In this age when everyone with a backpack proclaims him or herself a travel writer, it takes a book like this one to redefine the genre. The stories are personal and inviting, giving the reader not only a feeling of participation but leaving them with a memory of where they have just visited. This is just plain great travel writing." James Michael Dorsey, World Traveler and author of three travel collections.

Linda's first novel *Wai-nani: A Voice from Old Hawai'i* remains her proudest achievement. When she was 28, she dropped out of society and landed on the north shore of Kauai. She fell in love with the warmth and beauty of the Hawaiians and the nurturing Island life. Research for the novel became a beautiful 20-year obsession. The story inspired by feisty Ka'ahumanu, the favorite wife of Kamehameha the Great, follows his rise to power. She rose to be the most powerful woman in old Hawai'i and became responsible for ending the 2,000-year-old kapu system with the burning of the Gods.

Writing her second novel *The Cowgirl Jumped*

Over the Moon, was Linda's way of letting go of the riding world when an injury forced her to give up her mare. Her protagonist does everything Linda ever wanted to do on the back of a good horse. When Grand Prix jumper Gemcie McCauley takes a tumble on her Irish Hunter, it turns her world upside down. She heads for the High Sierra to find her balance and meets a lone fire lookout who gives her the courage to get back in the saddle and return to the jumping arena to beat the odds.

Embrace of the Wild, tells the story of Isabella Bird (1831-1904), a trailblazing travel writer who overcame personal challenges to become one of the most beloved figures of her time. After spending six transformational months in Hawai'i where she regained her strength, Bird set off on an 800-mile solo journey through the Rocky Mountains, where she fell in love with the rugged beauty of the region. In her book *A Lady's Life in the Rocky Mountains*, she vividly describes the breathtaking landscapes of Estes Park drawing tourists there from around the globe. Bird's rumored romance with the notorious Rocky Mountain Jim adds a touch of romance to the story.

Linda was honored to be selected to be the "Isabella Bird Expert" in the BBC docuseries *Trailblazers*. She is interviewed in the film by the three actresses re-enacting Isabella's journey in Colorado. The series aired in the UK in the winter of 2022 to popular acclaim.

Linda enjoys sharing PowerPoint presentations for her books via Zoom. A discounted price for book clubs with six or more members is available.

Linda's print books are available on her site www.LindaBallouAuthor.com. If you purchase on her site you receive a signed copy and free shipping anywhere in the U.S. Her books are also available in print and e-book everywhere books are sold. *The Cowgirl Jumped Over the Moon* and *Lost Angel Walkabout* audio books are available on Audible.

Previous Publication
of Works in This Collection

Jack London and Me - *Your Life is a Trip* magazine

Raven Brings the Sun - *Go Nomad* magazine

Bright Blossom in the Pacific - A 2020 Solas Award winner at Travel Tales Publications

Rafting in the Wake of Georgie White - *Real Travel Adventures* magazine

On the Road with Isabella Bird - A 2022 Solas Award winner at Travel Tales Publications

Meet Bennelong - NABBW - *On Metro* syndication

An African Odyssey - *Travelscope* magazine

The Enemy - *Ventura County Star* newspaper

Black Lake Sacha Lodge - *American Fitness* magazine

Romp Across the Top of the World - NABBW - *On Metro* syndication

Riding off the Grid - *Go World Travel* magazine, *Equitrekking* vacation guide and travel tips

Linda Ballou

Glacier Bay - Wildlife Haven - *ANG* newspaper

Forest in Your Boots - NABBW - *On Metro* syndication

Too Many Elephants in the Room - NABBW - (Updated 2023)

Que Station- *Travel World International* magazine

Was it Worth It – NABBW - *On Metro* syndication

Other Books in the Lost Angel Series
By Linda Ballou

Lost Angel in Paradise
Lost Angel Walkabout
Lost Angel Unleashed